D0108660

GILA

OTHER BOOKS BY GREGORY McNAMEE

NONFICTION

The Return of Richard Nixon (1989)

FICTION

Christ on the Mount of Olives (1990)

POETRY

Inconstant History (1989)

Philoktetes: A Verse Translation (1987)

COLLECTIONS

Named in Stone and Sky: An Arizona Anthology (1993)

Living in Words: Interviews from The Bloomsbury Review
(1988)

Resist Much, Obey Little: Some Notes on Edward Abbey
(1985, 1989)

GILA

The Life
and
Death
of
an
American
River

Gregory
McNamee

The Library of the American West
Herman J. Viola, Editor

ORION BOOKS
NEW YORK

Published by Orion Books, a division of Crown Publishers, Inc., 201 East 50th Street, New York, New York 10022. Member of the Crown Publishing Group.

Random House, Inc. New York, Toronto, London, Sydney, Auckland

ORION and colophon are trademarks of Crown Publishers, Inc.

Manufactured in the United States of America

Design by Nancy Kenmore

Library of Congress Cataloging-in-Publication Data

McNamee, Gregory.
    Gila : the life and death of an American river / Gregory McNamee.
       p. cm.
    Includes bibliographical references and index.
    1. Gila River (N.M. and Ariz.)—History. 2. Gila River Region
(N.M. and Ariz.)—History. I. Title.
    F817.G52M36   1993
    979.1'7—dc20   93-32938
                                           CIP

ISBN 0-517-59163-4

10 9 8 7 6 5 4 3 2 1

First Edition

Contents

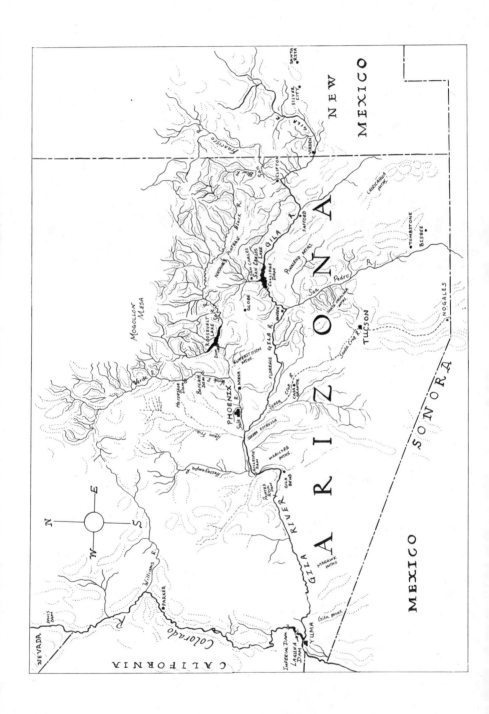

GILA

Water is the source of all things.
—THALES

1

GENESIS

September. It is late in the season for rain, but that has not kept a suddenly blackened sky from opening up here just a few minutes ago and pounding the mountains with hard drops of water the size of maize kernels. The deluge came on so suddenly, as storms in the Southwest will do, that it startled a pair of mule deer into head-over-heels flight down the talus slope that stretches precipitously, ever downward before me. Their dash was in vain, however. By the time they reached a sheltering overhang a few hundred yards away, the center of the rainsquall had whipped across the basin to the Continental Divide ten miles to the east, sending its water toward the Atlantic Ocean.

The approaching storm had set a nearby flock of ravens to cawing. They were acting out an ancient story: The raucous creaking of their voices is punishment for having cheated the first people out of a drink of water during a drought at the beginning of time. So goes an Indian

legend from the Sierra Madre of Mexico, its northernmost peaks forming blue mirages on the far horizon. When the weather is hot, as it
has been today, the birds are condemned to croak out their songs as
a badge of their thirst. Indeed, they fell silent the moment the water
began to drench the junipers in which they had gathered, as if to lend
further credence to the story. And now that the storm has gone, they
are back to making their old music.

Rivulets of water lace the high road out of the Mimbres River
valley from which I have just come. At one of these instant brooks a
diamondback rattlesnake has incautiously paused to bask and been run
over for its troubles; it lies squashed flat in the road, its triangular head
now a soft bullet of pulp. Some passerby has already stripped it of its
rattles, doubtless to grace a Southwest-style knickknack shelf. A golden
eagle, patiently floating on a bumpy thermal in the near sky, awaits
my departure to take in the lunch the unfortunate reptile affords.
Steam rises from every stone, the rainwater evaporating before the fire
of the newly uncovered sun.

The sky rumbles with distant thunder. The ravens raise up a new
cry within their thicket. These are primeval sounds, but all too easily
overcome. The nearest city—an overgrown town, really, of ten thousand inhabitants or so—is forty miles of rough road away. But even
in this fastness, once a nursery of silence, the rhythms of nature are
broken by the insistent whine of lumber trucks shifting up the long
grade to the Springerville sawmill and, less frequently, by the roar of
jet fighters from airbases three hundred miles away, which comb the
hills for targets in what the pilots call Indian Country. Across the wide
valley to the immediate north lies the nation's oldest federally designated wilderness area. Even it affords no escape from the cacophonous
music of the American machine age.

Now the last rain clouds are beginning to part, and my vantage
point here atop Copperas Peak at last yields the view I have come to

The middle fork of the Gila River, with the Mogollon Mountains in the background. (Photograph by the author)

see: the rushing headwaters of the Gila (pronounced *HEE-luh*) River, three streams that pour down from the surrounding highlands of southwestern New Mexico and unite two thousand sheer feet below me. The vista is dizzying. "Don't go into the Gila if you're scared of heights," a waitress in Silver City had said fifteen years ago, on my first visit here, after watching me puzzle over a topographic map. She had a point. These streams and their feeders arise in springs and ice caves atop towering ranges—the Mogollon, Black, and Pinos Altos mountains—that ring the Gila Basin to the immediate west of the Continental Divide. The vertiginous roads that lead over them and down to the water are an acrophobiac's worst nightmare.

Rain, sacred rain. It is a precious resource in these uplands, a thousand miles from the nearest ocean. It is still more precious in the arid desert that surrounds the mountains. Owing to accidents of wind flow and geology, these mountains receive at best twenty-three inches of precipitation a year, a quantity that, say, New Orleans might receive in a few days of summer. At the Gila's end, six hundred miles to the west along the solar flats of the Arizona desert near Yuma, the rainfall often may not exceed three inches a year; the region is one of the most arid in North America. There the most memorable storms are not of water but of sand, the violent simoon of cowboy song and Hollywood oater. The exotic word comes from the Arabic *samúm*, meaning "poison," and anyone who has ridden out such a storm knows how fitting the derivation is. In the pages of Herodotus you will find the story of a Libyan army that marched off two and a half millennia ago into the Sahara to find and subdue the lord of these storms. The expedition never returned, "disappearing, in battle array, with drums and cymbals beating, into the red cloud of swirling sand." So far no army has been buried by a homegrown Sonoran Desert sandstorm, but the scouring winds have left morbid monuments enough. The British explorer and spy Raphael Pumpelly, who traveled the river's course in 1862, found this eerie spectacle:

> *We were approaching the Tinajas Altas, the only spot where, for a distance of nearly 120 miles, water might at times be found.*
>
> *It was a brilliant moonlit night. On our left rose a lofty sierra, its fantastic sculpturing weird even in the moonlight. Suddenly we saw strange forms indefinable in the distance. As we came nearer our horses became uneasy, and we saw before us animals standing on each side of, and facing the trail. It was a long avenue between rows of mummified cattle, horses and sheep.*

The vast boneyard of the Southwest is governed meteorologically by the swift air currents of the North Pacific, their actions tempered seasonally by tropical systems to the south. The prevailing winds bring little water to the desert from the high mountains that shade the Pacific Coast; these mountain ranges block the flow of air and milk the clouds of most of the moisture they bear, giving rise to the so-called rainshadow effect on the leeward side. Such scant rain as the desert uplands manage to wring from the great wind rivers passing above them—the process is called orographic precipitation, and any cloud is fair game at any time of the year—is a blessing indeed, especially at this late date, weeks beyond the customary end of the ironically named monsoon season.

More than the rain, there are the annual snowfalls, which are scenic if not terribly heavy in the Gila uplands. The writer John Jerome has noted that snow "is a storehouse, more effective than all the dams in history, for the single resource that powers industry, sustains agriculture, maintains our very life—our water supply." The Southwest is not known for the bitterness of its winters, but even when the temperature on the desert floor reaches a hundred degrees, often by the middle of April, the higher elevations retain their great snowfields, gradually releasing them in the form of flowing water by the beginning of summer. Such is the case in good years, at any rate, after a season's accumulation of five or six feet of snow. You can tell a bad year in these parts by how loudly the ski-resort operators complain that business is off. At the beginning of the 1980s, some had almost convinced the federal government to seed the skies with silver iodide pellets and thus coax the white manna from heaven, the rhythms of nature be damned.

Without that rain and snow much of the interior West would quickly be depopulated. Cities like Phoenix, Tucson, and Los Angeles—all dependent in some measure on the Gila—would quickly be swallowed up by the sands. (The modern descendants of the aboriginal desert peoples doubtless would not think this such a bad thing.) The scenario is entirely plausible, although boosters of the boomtown Sun-belt do not like to admit it. The rivers of the Southwest "fail"—in the parlance of the hydrologists—every five years or so. The climato-logical record of the last thousand years is peppered with instances of twenty- and thirty-year drought cycles—enough to send European America reeling from the arid lands as surely as earlier civilizations dissolved before the natural world's realities, climate being one of the great motors of evolution and of social change and not especially re-sponsive to our feeble tampering.

The rainfall that now evaporates, steaming around my ankles, could not have exceeded a sixteenth of an inch. Still, it was enough to stir these mountains to new life. And for the time being, there is water enough in these highlands to sustain a rich mantle of scrub oak, juniper, pinyon, ponderosa pine ("of all the pines," John Muir said, "this one gives the finest music to the winds"), wild cherry, alder, aspen, Engelmann spruce, mahogany, and cottonwood. There is enough to host the migratory waterbirds that dot the river below, the ospreys and kingfishers and geese, the egrets, grebes, rails, and galli-nules. There is enough to feed the coyotes, mountain lions, jaguarun-dis, ocelots, and bobcats that still dwell in the mountains and box canyons of this high country, careful to avoid contact with humans from which they would surely emerge the loser. There is enough to support the great (and sometimes too large) populations of deer and elk. But not enough to support the too-large population of humans that has filled the desert since the end of the Second World War.

Were the river still alive along its entire course, it would nurture humans and more. Until recently—almost within living memory—the Gila and its tributaries formed the most important river system in the Southwestern heartland, draining an area of 250,000 square miles, larger than the nation of France. It marked the boundaries between peoples, contained invaders from north and south, and was an avenue for communication of biological and cultural information. Without the river the great prehistoric civilizations of the Southwest would not have risen. Without it the histories of Spain, Mexico, and the United States would have been markedly different, and markedly poorer.

We owe the river honor. Instead, we continue to destroy it.

Most of the rivers that now cross the earth are infants in geological time. The Colorado River cut through the Grand Canyon only in the last three and a half million years, carving into two billion years' accumulation of rock at the rate of one meter every five hundred years. The Mississippi is much younger, assuming its present meandering course during the last period of worldwide glaciation, which ended only ten thousand years ago. Even today, the Mississippi seeks a new path to the sea through the estuary of the Atchafalaya River, a hundred miles west of the river's present outlet south of New Orleans. The Gila is an older but still comparatively youthful flow, dating in its more or less present form to a few million years. But its course was laid out by a series of ancestral flows that stretched back to at least seventy million years before the present (B.P.).

The basin and range province that embraces the Gila drainage and defines the North American interior from northern Nevada to central Mexico is one of the most thoroughly studied regions of the world, probed for two centuries by geologists and prospectors on the hunt for petroleum, minerals, and precious gems. It is defined by a pattern of generally northwest-to-southeast mountain chains that are punctuated by broad valleys of loosely packed sediment, all caused by a series of pull-apart extension faults, as if the earth's mantle beneath were rushing in separate directions. The distribution of these faults is so regular that the crest-and-trough arrangement seems very nearly deliberate, as if a childlike god had scattered these building-block mountains across the giant playroom of the mountain West at the dawn of time.

The regularity stems from well-known physical processes. The surface crust of the earth is borne along on convection currents arising from its fiery center, made up of iron, sulphur, and silicates. This crust is made up of large plates that float on the denser viscous matter, or mantle, below them. Huge bodies of land ride on the backs of these plates but most of the present continents, like North America, are fragmented among several plates. Where those plates collide—along the California coast, say—is the violent arena of landmass-building, of earthquakes and volcanoes, of the birth of great mountains.

One chain, the Ancestral Rockies, pushed its way up out of the earth nearly three hundred and fifty million years B.P., born of a massive upthrust of mantle material. The exposed new ground was cracked and twisted by massive subterranean forces, carved by rivers and encroaching oceans, and eventually weathered away to nothing, recapitulating geological processes as old as the planet itself. By 300 million years B.P., the 20,000-foot-high Ancestral Rockies had been eroded to the horizon. Remaining layers of the mountains still underlie the Great Plains, but their memory, so to speak, was imprinted in the earth for a succeeding generation of mountains to revive, and the present Rockies, the southernmost reaches of which take in the headwaters of the Gila, generally follow their ancestors' course.

The mountain-building action on the North American continent shifted eastward, giving rise to the comparatively ancient Appalachian chain; the inaptly named New River, arising in the mountains of West Virginia, is in fact the oldest river on earth, predating the second oldest, the Nile, by millions of years. The continental mass that makes up our present West, at one time positioned alongside the earth's equator somewhere near the present south-central Pacific, lay under a giant inland sea bordered by swamplands, as evidenced today by extensive dinosaur fossil beds, petrified forests of ancient coniferous trees that were two hundred feet tall, and underground lakes of oil and, even more precious, of fossil water.

One hundred and fifty million years B.P., the area of what today is the Gila drainage, along with most of what now constitutes western North America, lay beneath a vast saline lake contained by a block of mountains along the Pacific Coast. Into this sea were deposited the grains of riverborne and windborne sand, which sunk to the bottom, along with the bodies of fishes, insects, and marine invertebrates—fossils of ancestral jellyfish, horseshoe crabs, and dragonflies figure prominently in this region's exposed rock strata—to form chemically hardened layers of earth that reached thicknesses of a mile or more. When the sea dried up, these layers of sandstone, limestone, and shale—no longer suppressed by the weight of water—rose up as exposed land and in turn were worn down and molded into weird patterns by the earth's forces of wind and water, sometimes to be reborn as an isolated upthrust of mineral-rich metamorphic rock.

A period of intense volcanism beginning about 70 million years B.P. gave birth to the earth's great mountain systems of today, including the Himalayas, the giant massifs of Antarctica, the European Alps, and the pan-American Cordillera, the last of which embraces the Rockies, the Sierra Madre of Mexico, and the Andes of South America. (If you look at a physical map of the Americas you will see that these seemingly distinct ranges form a nearly unbroken chain eight thousand miles long.) This great period of mountain building, which lasted nearly thirty million years, was accompanied by widespread climatic change. Among other events, Antarctica froze, lowering the level of the oceans as billions of gallons of water were locked in ice and causing most of the world's inland seas to dry up as their waters sought the lower elevations. With the disappearance of the great Carboniferous-era sea that had lapped over much of the interior West came a dying off of perhaps 80 percent of the existing life-forms, among them thousands of varieties of ferns and mosses, fish, and reptiles. This diversity of life has not been equaled since.

In the region of the Gila, which began its life as a southerly outlet of an ancient series of seas, the last waters drained by way of the Río Grande rift valley to the east—a deeply cut fault that will likely, in a few million years to come, widen to admit a new ocean into the Great Plains—and the Salton Trough to the west, which cut south twenty million years ago to form the Gulf of California. This sink eventually shades north into the best-known geological feature in the United States, the San Andreas Fault system.

In its final period of uplifting, at the end of the so-called Laramide Orogeny, the Mogollon Highlands rose to roughly their present height of nearly eleven thousand feet from eight thousand feet. As they did, they blocked off a vast lake to the north, now the Plains of San Agustín, where an ancient volcano exploded with such force that pieces of the cone were hurled scores of miles away, scattering the landscape with great chunks of fire-twisted rock. (Such rocks can be seen along Interstate 40 near Grants, New Mexico, and in the great volcanic fields along Interstate 8 near Tacna, Arizona.) Hundreds of other volcanoes dotted the region, and many Arizonan and New Mexican highways provide views of unmistakable cinder cones—silent reminders of the forces of the earth.

As the land broadens in the western lowlands beyond Florence, Arizona, where roughly half the river's course is run, the mountains become fewer and smaller. They are also more ancient; the oldest mountains of the Papaguería, as southwestern Arizona has been called, are made up of Precambrian schists, gneiss, and granites, along with more recent shales, tephras, and micas, all of which leave in their decay a complex cryptogamic soil, rich in chemicals that bind the rough sand and reduce erosion. Separating these jagged mountain chains are vast

The lava chaos along the lower Gila, near Dateland, Arizona.
(Photograph by the author)

plains of desert, pavement, alkali flats, and a great lava chaos that collectively make up some of the continent's wildest landscapes.

Wherever they lay, as the mountains aged they shed their loose rocks, which accumulated at their bases in great alluvial fans, or *bajadas*, and were carried off by rainwater and gravity into the valleys. Underlain by ancient impermeable clays and granite, these valleys—or grabens—filled to a depth of more than a mile, forming a gravel-bottomed bowl that eventually filled nearly to the top with rainwater. This abundance of underground reservoirs fed the Gila and other Southwestern rivers as surely as the rain and snow, and allowed the development of the human civilizations that would one day subdue them.

Somewhere within our genetic being we bear the ancestral memory of these long-distant geological events. All the known cultures of the world relate tales of a shaking earth, of great deluges, of cataclysm. Our forebears witnessed the birth of mountains. They saw great floods as well, and their reports constitute the world's most ancient literatures. Thanks to the work of anthropologists and folklorists, many of these stories have survived, even when the societies that elaborated them have not.

In 1936, traveling among the peoples of the upper Gila, an ethnologist named Grenville Goodwin recorded a remarkable flood legend that was patiently related to him by storyteller Anna Price, a San Carlos Apache. As surely as any scientific rendering, it summarizes the complex geological and ecological history of the Gila River. The *t'us* of which she speaks, the ark of the first people, is a water container made of woven reeds or grasses and subsequently daubed in mud or sealed with pine pitch.

> *Long long ago people were living on this earth. Then Tanager came to them and said that the ocean was going to come over this country and cover all their homes. Tanager came to where two boys were living with their mother and told them they must build a great big* t'us, *so that all three could go inside it when the ocean came and save themselves. He told them to weave this* t'us *out of brush and to pitch it all over outside, so it would not leak. So these people started in to work on the* t'us. *Tanager went among the other camps and told them to do the same way, to make a big* t'us *for themselves to get into. But they would not*

believe him and just laughed when he told them. "What's the matter with you that you want us to make t'us for ourselves to get in when the ocean comes? We do not believe the ocean is ever coming here," they said. But those two boys went ahead and made a big t'us as Tanager had told them. When it was finished they could stand up inside it and there was just room enough for them.

Then Tanager said to them, "I want you to gather some wood and put it inside your t'us. Also put some dirt inside and some food. Put in lots of yucca fruit and corn and sunflower seeds." So the brothers started to do as they were told. They ground up lots of sunflower seeds and lots of corn. It took them two days to get all this food ready. Tanager told them to make a flat rock to put over the mouth of the t'us, to seal it. So the brothers ground down a flat rock to just the right size. When all was ready the brothers got inside the big t'us. Then Tanager told them, "I want you to seal that rock on with pitch, over the mouth of the t'us so it won't leak. I will know when the water will be all gone again. When it is all gone I will pick up this t'us and carry it some place and set it down on the ground. Then you must come out of the t'us again."

The sea started to come to this place and cover all the land. Then the brothers went in to their big t'us. When the water got to the camps of the people who would not believe Tanager, they saw the water and believed. They came running over to where the brothers were in their t'us and wanted to get in, but there was no room for them. Some of the women cried to the brothers to take their children inside and save them, but they could not do it. Then people climbed up into the trees to try and save themselves, but the water kept on rising and some of the trees fell over. These people were all drowned and washed away. . . .

Now the water started to sink into the ground and go away. When the water was gone, Tanager set the t'us down by the side of the river. The people inside it came out. All the earth was changed. All the mountains and trees and plants and rocks, everything had been washed away. At that place there was only level, sandy country with nothing growing on it at all. . . .

Then Bear came there. "I hear you have a hard time and are starving to death. That's why I have come. I have lots of food on me," he said to those people. He shook himself and out of him fell xuctco'; he shook himself again and out fell xucdilko' he, then xucntsazi, then xucts'ise [all these are edible cacti], yucca fruit, piñon nuts. "Now I have brought lots of food for you people," Bear said. He shook again and out fell juniper berries, Gambel's oak acorns, Emory's oak acorns, manzanita berries, tc'idnk'u' je [sumac], gadts'agi [juniper], na' djilba' ye [edible seed], and 'id'a' dilko [acorns]. All these that Bear gave us are the ones growing on the earth today. . . .

There was only a little water left in the t'us (not the big one) that they had brought with them, and so they went to Beaver Old Man to ask him to help them get water. When they got to where he was living, they found him lying down, and asked him, prayed to him, to help them get water. "Well, there are lots of you people here. How am I going to find water for you?" he said. The children were crying for water, they were so thirsty. "Well, give me a t'us and I will see if I can get some water for you," said Beaver Old Man. So they gave him a t'us and he started off. He was back right away with the water. He said he had found water in some pools on the rocks. With this water the people boiled some corn stew for themselves. The children also drank lots of water. But still the t'us of water stayed full. After a little while the children of Beaver Old Man came to where the people

The Gila River in flood, near its confluence with the Colorado River, March 1992. (Photograph by the author)

were and told them their father had lied about the water. "He did not get the water where he said he got it. He got it right at his camp where the springs are coming out. There are springs right there," they said. Beaver is the one that the people prayed to get them water, lots of it, and he is the one who started the water flowing in Black River and Gila River and in springs and rivers all over the earth.

In this primeval time the water began to flow—indeed, torrents of it out of a *t'us* that could not be drained—from the Mogollon Highlands to a distant cut in the hills bordering the great Colorado River. As it bore its way through sandstones and granites, overcoming the obstacles in its way, it developed its present stream flow, a course marked by turbulent, narrow riffles alternating with slower stretches and still, deep pools in roughly equal proportion. It conquered mountain after mountain, etched its course into the serest sands, to find its outlet at the far-off sea. As it wandered, the river filled with white salmon, with native trout, with mosquitofish, with a dozen other native fish species of which only half survive today. (Given the disastrous effects of sheet erosion on streams across America, including the Gila, the baby-boom generation may be one of the last to see native fish outside a hatchery.) It became a great biological treasure house, a role that it served for millions of years.

If the river carried a name then, it was known only to its maker. Since then it has borne many appellations, most of them lost to time. Many standard references give the origin of the present name as a Mimbres Apache word meaning "spider," an erroneous but nice enough conceit, given the tangled tracery of the headwaters, as seemingly random as a black widow's web. When the Spanish conquistadores and missionaries arrived at the great river four and a half centuries ago, at first they bestowed upon it the descriptive name Río Azul—"Blue River"—since applied to an Arizona tributary. Later clerics gave it the religiously charged names Río de los Apostoles—"River of the Apostles"—and Río del Nombre de Jesus—"River of the Name of Jesus"—as if to fix their newly imported faith upon the land itself. At the point where the Gila joins the Colorado River, a Spanish soldier heard a Yuma Indian refer to the inflowing stream as Hahquahsaael, or "salty water running," and wrestled the term into his report as best he could: Xíla. The name stuck in a simplified form: Gila.

The Spanish soldier's rendering is but one of countless linguistic misunderstandings that dot the map of the Southwest; our vocabularies have been wrong from the start. Historically, the Gila has been one of the continent's preeminent desert rivers, but *desert* isn't quite right, either. *Desert*: The English term and its Latin ancestors mean, at heart, "an uninhabited or abandoned place," as in the desert isle Robinson Crusoe found himself stranded on, a place as if depopulated after some terrible catastrophe. The Europeans who first saw the great arid expanses of northern Mexico and what is now the southwestern United States used a familiar term, ignoring the large populations of indigenous peoples who made their home in the dry lands, as well as the astonishing variety of flora and fauna that had adapted to these extremes of heat and aridness, the preeminent characteristics of the region. Perhaps they could not have perceived the place otherwise. The invaders saw these lands as obstacles to be surmounted, as a land to be subdued. From the canyon-carved highlands of the Mogollon Rim to the scorched plains at the river's end, their descendants followed that same path.

Wrong though it is, the word *desert* will have to do to describe the Gila's compass. But even after the depredations of the last two hundred years, the so-called desert is full of life: pumas and coyotes, elk and antelope, mule deer and pronghorn, eagles and hawks, snakes, lizards, beetles, spiders, ants. Bear's generous gifts to the Gila's ancient inhabitants were but a small sample of the abundant plant and animal life in this supposed desolation. No place along the Gila lacks a wide variety of life-forms; the ecosystemic patches—the river bottoms and highlands and the desert basins and grasslands—that make up its drainage harbor nearly the full range of plant types in the Southwest. Almost all the animals of the desert, too, depend on the Gila for their existence, adjusting themselves to an environment where water is scarce and unpredictable.

The continued survival of these plants and animals is at issue now. For well over half of the river's course—its vast groundwater lakes all but drained—the Gila carries water only in years of extreme precipitation, when the various diversion channels and dams that dot its path cannot contain the flood. Some mapmakers acknowledge this truth by marking the lower Gila with dot-and-dash blue lines—cartographic code for the dead—but most atlases continue the tragic fiction that great waters still lace through the intermountain West, awaiting millions of new conquistadores.

Given its own lead, the land forms itself in imperceptibly slow ways. We know but can scarcely comprehend the antiquity of the ground on which we stand. We know, too, the elements of its life span—the wind with its blasts of sand and water, the gravity that sends mountains tumbling down as surely as it bends us in old age, the great internal forces that resurrect the earth for still another cycle of growth and decay.

Knowing as much as we do, the land seldom has its own way. The work of millions of years of geological change, of weathering and uplifting and abrasion, can be undone in a few minutes by a bulldozer, a concrete form, a blasting cap. For millions of years, the course of the Gila River must have seemed a manifestation of the primeval Garden of Eden—another hallowed, faraway desert paradise between rushing waters, another deeply implanted memory. In scarcely a hundred years, a rapacious industrial civilization betrayed that eons-long promise of a bit of heaven on earth.

And as with all our terrestrial paradises, Eden is now lost.

*There were once men capable of inhabiting
a river without disrupting the
harmony of its life.*
—ALDO LEOPOLD

2

THE TRANSIT
OF EDEN

The river coursed through mountain to valley to desert floor for millennia. It kept its own rhythms, varying its bounty with the rain that blew in along the horse latitudes and north from the still-forming Pacific Coast and the far-off Gulf of Mexico. Over time it established a certain regularity. The Gila and its principal tributaries—from east to west, the present San Francisco, San Carlos, San Pedro, Salt/Verde, Agua Fria, and Hassayampa rivers—predictably carried some three to four million acre feet of water a year. For a desert country, that is a huge blessing: an acre foot is about 345,000 gallons, or enough water to cover an acre of land to the depth of a foot or sustain an average American family of four for a year. (The same acre foot over the same time would support a hundred Somalis, who value water for what it truly is.) By way of contrast, the modern Colorado carries between ten and twelve million acre feet of water a year, a tenth of the Mississippi's annual load.

Some years drought overtook the desert, and the river failed. Some years, the sky imparted a surfeit of rainwater and snow; when it did, the river left its narrow banks and surged over the surrounding floodplain, enriching the normally dry belt along the river with fresh deposits of mineral-rich and nutrient-laden alluvium, a process ecologists call "flood pulse." That regular enrichment, analogous to the work of a careful gardener, in time developed into a series of bountiful ecosystems. Along the banks of the river great forests grew, made up mostly of cottonwood, willow, sycamore, boxelder, walnut, hackberry, and mesquite. Near the confluences of tributaries and along side-streams formed palustrine wetlands—treelined swamps situated within an arid zone—and *ciénegas*, or marshes, called after the Spanish *cién aguas*, "hundred waters." Bankside plants fed on the river, and they guarded it as well by locking as much as two-thirds of its annual load into their root systems, shielding it from evaporation under the usually fierce sun.

The richness of plant life attracted an abundance of animal life. The riparian thickets swarmed with countless species in a textbook example of a food chain, with myriad small organisms sustaining a smaller number of larger ones in an inverted pyramid pattern. There are more worms than there are birds, for example, in any balanced ecosystem, and fewer animals that feed on birds, and fewer animals still that rely on those predators for their daily bread. The aggregate number of animals that sheltered alongside the Gila was at least a hundred times greater than in the surrounding desert. We have no reliable way of estimating the density of animal life when humans first arrived at the banks of the Gila, but considering the quantity and variety of bones found in sites associated with the earliest human habitations, it must have been far denser than at any time since.

Just when aboriginal people came to the continent has been a matter of scholarly speculation for centuries. Received wisdom has it that they came during the last major ice age glaciation some 12,000 years B.P., when the Bering land bridge connected northern Siberia and Alaska. This model assumes a social organization that would have been prepared for mass exodus, and it allows little room for the notion of a gradual immigration over centuries.

But there have been challenges to this view. Recently a team of scholars has been studying Paleo-Indian migration to the New World by looking at historical linguistics, blood types, and dental patterns—seemingly disparate matters that point to waves of humans traveling across the land bridge for far longer than had been suspected, almost all of them from the Lake Baikal region. Maverick scholar Julian Hayden argues that Cro-Magnons drifted into the Americas at least a quarter of a million years ago, only to die off along with their Old World cousins. So far the academy has ignored the admittedly ambiguous evidence that Hayden presents from sites in Baja California, Mexico, and Texas, near the confluence of the Pecos River and the Río Grande.

More recently, archaeologist Richard MacNeish has been excavating two sites in the Pintado and Pendejo caves on the MacGregor Firing Range, part of the vast Fort Bliss military reservation outside of El Paso, Texas. In these sites, lying only two hundred miles east of the Gila's headwaters, MacNeish has found the flint-butchered bones of *Equus niobrensis*, a large horse that roamed the Great Plains until 30,000 B.P. Other bones identified as the long-extinct Aztlán rabbit and extinct miniature Eohippus, or "dawn horse," found in association with human remains push the dates of occupation back to at least 40,000 B.P., or about the time the first aborigines crossed into Australia, which at that time was joined to Asia by another land bridge. And there is good reason to believe that other sites in the arid Southwest will extend the presence of humans in America much farther back in antiquity.

For now, the earliest evidence of human settlement in the vicinity of the Gila River comes from two sites in southeastern Arizona, the Lehner and Naco killing grounds. Here, jutting from the banks of two arroyos that are near what was the shore of a 120-square-mile inland sea that dried up only eight millennia ago, were found the bones of mastodons and Columbian mammoths—elephantine creatures that were the largest terrestrial species on the North American continent. Close by, their discoverers located so-called Folsom points—stone weapons wielded by Paleo-Indians who hunted the animals in these places more than twelve thousand years ago.

They came to a region that looked far different from how it does today. The middle elevations of the Sonoran Desert, now largely patches of grassland and prickly pear, were carpeted with ponderosa pine, alligator juniper, and other temperate forest plants now found only above seven thousand feet. The annual rainfall was more than forty inches, about the average Iowa receives today, while the mountains received nearly twice that amount. At this time, the area that now constitutes New York City lay under a sheet of ice several hundred feet thick, while active glaciers gnawed at the highlands of New Mexico and Arizona, contributing shreds of rock to the debris-filled valley floors.

The land was the province of large animals that have since disappeared from North America: the tapir, sloth, dire wolf, four-pronged antelope, mastodon, and its shaggy highland cousin, the Columbian mammoth, and what surely sent terror through the first humans to encounter it: a giant bear that stood ten feet tall at the shoulder, far larger than any modern bear. All these creatures offered quite a larder, and the earliest archaeological sites suggest that the Paleo-Indians availed themselves freely of the bounty. At Ventana Cave, Arizona, within two or three days' walk of the lower Gila, excavator Emil Haury catalogued evidence of their protein-rich diet: the bones of prairie dogs, otters, camels, tapirs, short-faced bears, tigers, deer, badgers, wolves, an extinct jaguar called *Felis atrox*, horses, and bison lay intermingled with scrapers, flint projectile points, and choppers in testimony to a prehistoric barbecue that seemingly would not quit.

But it did. One by one the Pleistocene megafauna began to disappear, setting off a tide of New World extinctions that could not be stemmed. Some of the large animals were hunted out of existence, fallen before a new species of predator with unbounded faith in a continued food supply. Others were squeezed out of their ecological niches by a changing climate. As the last ice age at last began its retreat some ten thousand years ago, in a period of global warming, the face of the continent began to change. Along the Gila the great forests began to retreat up the mountainsides, leaving only vestigial species like the kachina daisy and giving way to the present associations of trees that thrive on relatively little water. The drier lowlands became host to the cacti that are now characteristic of Southwestern deserts— plants that evolved in the tropical rainforests of Central America, spread northward, and adapted to a drier climate by extracting water from an occasionally rain-wetted soil and storing it for later use.

The density of animal life diminished, and with it the number of permanent human occupations in the desert: the fewer prey, after all, the fewer predators. After 7500 B.P., the Paleo-Indians moved from streamside caves into the now-parched lowlands and adapted to a nomadic way of life, traveling over great distances in search of migrating herds of herbivores. As they did, they learned to rely more on plant foods, laying the foundation for the ethnobotanical tradition of their descendants. As is true of most nomadic peoples, the Paleo-Indians left little behind; gone were the days of the great bone heaps and scrap piles of flaked stone. But if you wander out into the remoter parts of the desert today, in places where plows have not yet touched the brittle earth, you will occasionally happen on fire rings—rough circles of stone that, humble though they are, mark the first Native American architecture. These signs of civilization constituted the first long-term alteration of the landscape by human hands.

The Paleo-Indians left other marks. To drive game animals into stream bottoms or other confines where they could be easily taken, the desert people took to burning large swaths of lowland forest, clearing the ground and allowing the spread of native grasses—plants that had come into being at about the time the earliest parts of the Gila did—from their riparian habitat onto the valley floor. In the lowlands, these grasses—tobosa and black grama—would feed the last of the bison in the Southwest; they and their highland cousin, pinyon grass, would later serve as a lure for European cattle. The practice must have come out of long observation of the effects of natural wildfire, which occurred about every seven years, on the Gila's ecosystems. Fire, the aboriginal people understood, acts as a sort of surface-world antibody, removing dead and decaying plants and recharging the soil with nutrients. It also opens habitat for wildlife while at the same time encouraging new growth, and these hungry ancestors must have also hoped that their sacred fire would scare up new prey as it burned. Smokey the Bear notwithstanding, when fire is allowed into an ecosystem, the results are almost entirely beneficial; when it is not, decayed wood and undergrowth accumulates as a great kindling pile, with eventual results like the spectacular fires in Yellowstone National Park in 1988 and Oakland, California, in 1991.

Bands of Paleo-Indians eventually made their way into the mountains of the upper Gila, where previously it had been too cold to settle. The last of the glaciers had only just retreated from the river's headwaters, and the cobble-choked streams provided abundant water and food, both vegetable and animal. They must have liked what they saw, because the Paleo-Indians stayed. Over the centuries, they developed a solid, permanent civilization whose remains still dot the landscapes of the upper Gila.

Called the "Cochise culture" after the great (and ethnically un-related) Apache leader of the nineteenth century, these people gained an important advantage two millennia ago. From traders who traveled along the Sierra Madrean cordillera came the seeds of *Zea mexicana*, or teosinte, a wild grass first domesticated as *Zea mays* in the Valley of Mexico some five thousand years earlier—or so many archaeologists believe—at roughly the same time wheat was domesticated in the Levant and rice in East Asia. This floury-kerneled native corn required a growing period of only ninety to a hundred days, and its adaptation allowed the Cochise people to escape a cycle of feast and famine.

The Cochise culture, now agricultural, shifted subtly; its people became more sedentary, and by about A.D. 200 they began to erect ever larger, more permanent structures along the valleys of the headwater basin. These changes heralded others, among them likely a fixed social hierarchy and an organized religion with a priestly class. These are matters of the deepest conjecture, but the architectural patterns of the culture, its later stages now designated the Mogollon, suggest that a handful of people enjoyed the choicer bits of real estate, close to perennial water and scenic views, as is the case of the present Gila Cliff Dwellings National Monument, where water and crystallized salts acted in concert to break the caprock and form a cozy natural shelter, while others lived more simply in outlying settlements along tributary streams. The Mogollon necropolis near present-day Springerville, Arizona—a network of catacombs unlike any other prehistoric cemetery in the Southwest—indicates this people's regard for religious observance, if not for the afterlife itself.

Squash, beans, and peppers followed teosinte into the Mogollon culture area, and they quickly became just as important in the larder. The Mogollon now practiced a form of swidden agriculture, in which they regularly burned forest undergrowth and planted seeds in the hot

*Mogollon apartments at the Gila Cliff Dwellings National Monument,
near the river's headwaters.* (Photograph by the author)

ashes, emulating the effects of lightning-caused forest fires. This was
much more sound ecologically than the slash-and-burn agriculture of
the neighboring Anasazi, the northerly people who built such sprawl-
ing cities as Chaco Canyon and Mesa Verde, practically deforesting the
lowland Four Corners region in the process. Swidden agriculture encouraged the regeneration of the forest through more or less random
site selection and the tendency of Mogollon farmers to clear small plots
among thriving stretches of woodland.

The Gila gave the Mogollon people all they needed. A 1947 campaign of excavations at Bat Cave, New Mexico, near the headwaters
of the river on the southern end of the bowl-like Plains of San Agustín, provided evidence that the Mogollon enjoyed an astonishing
range of foodstuffs at most times of the year. (It was there that the

first Southwestern maize was discovered as well.) Remains recovered from Mogollon Village, on the east bank of the San Francisco River, showed that even the outlying settlements apparently were fat and happy much of the time: the people who lived there dined on badgers, raccoons, coyotes, red foxes, mountain lions, wood rats, mule deer, bison, turkeys, great horned owls, hawks, and ducks, along with corn, beans, squash, amaranth greens, and wild berries, a feast that contemporary Europeans would rightly have envied.

The Mogollon were sophisticated, at least, in ways that might have surprised the invading descendants of those Europeans. In the late stages of their culture they were renowned for the black-on-white painted pottery they made of riverbank clay, examples of which have been found as far south as central Mexico and as far west as the Pacific coast of California. They had an advanced knowledge of engineering, too: Captain B. D. Gaillard, an early American explorer, reported finding on the river's headwaters a Mogollon dam that "consisted of giant earthworks 3½ miles long and 22 to 24 feet high, involving in its construction the handling of 800,000 to 1,000,000 cubic yards of material." A cattle rancher later destroyed the dam to reclaim meadowland for grazing.

To that civil-engineering skill we might add a complex understanding of local geography. A Mogollon site near Sanchez, in the area of the so-called Gila Box of eastern Arizona, contains a petroglyph, or rock painting, that scholars have interpreted as a map of the entire eastern Gila watershed. The claim is not at all far-fetched, considering the elaborate intercontinental trade networks that obtained in the ancient Americas. After all, the Pueblo Indian demigod Kokopelli, the humpbacked flute player, has his origins in the highlands of Incan Peru, thousands of miles distant. And Mount Lemmon, which towers above the middle San Pedro Valley, was sacred not only to the nearby Tohono O'odham but also to the Diegueño and Luiseño peoples who lived along the southern California shore, nearly five hundred miles distant.

The Mogollon culture was "nuclear" in the sense that from it the arts of pottery making and agriculture spread throughout the greater Southwest. It influenced architecture as well: the early Mogollon pithouses evolved into kivas—subterranean ceremonial chambers that remain central elements of Puebloan religious practice today. Despite its importance to the development of the prehistoric Southwest, however, the Mogollon culture ultimately took more than it gave. It began to fade before overpowering Anasazi influences, and after A.D. 1150 it seems to have lost most of the cultural traits that defined it as a distinct people.

The river gave birth to other societies. Along the middle Gila near the present site of Coolidge Dam, a people archaeologists have yet to name formed a society devoted nearly exclusively to the cultivation of agave, a succulent plant that provides fiber, food, and building materials. The culture did not persist, and we know comparatively little about the lives of its people; the few tangible remains are a series of agricultural terraces on the slopes of the Pinaleño Mountains, visible only from the air. The people were likely absorbed into the nascent Hohokam culture, whose domain lay along the river to the west, but it left as its legacy a tradition of agave use that has endured among the peoples of the Gila until modern times.

The Patayan culture, ancestral to the Yumas at the confluence of the Gila and Colorado rivers, also represents something of a blank in regional history. Such material evidence for the Patayan as exists often lies buried under meters of silt, for they built their simple brush huts on floodplains, where they were periodically swept away by rising water. The Patayan was the last prehistoric Southwestern culture to take up agriculture, at about A.D. 700, and that agriculture was based exclusively on floodwater farming, relying on the rivers' exceeding their banks annually. When the rivers did not do so, as was often the case, the people starved; and in any event, floodwater farming allows only one maize crop a year, unlike the two crops the Mogollon and Hohokam enjoyed through irrigation. The Patayan were in every respect the poor cousins of the ancient Southwest, and their descendants fared little better.

By contrast, the Hohokam culture of the middle Gila lived on easy street. Basing their economy on a sophisticated knowledge of hydraulic engineering unequaled in the New World—and indeed rivaling those of Mesopotamia and ancient Rome—the Hohokam built an elaborate network of irrigation canals, some eight miles long, along the great plain that stretches westward from North Butte and South Butte, near Florence, to a point east of present-day Gila Bend, Arizona. These hundreds of miles of canals allowed for year-round farming, and they provided the Hohokam a comfortable material culture that approached ostentation.

The Hohokam, according to archaeologist Emil W. Haury, came into the Gila drainage as "a fully blown culture," perhaps having migrated north from Mesoamerica by way of the western Sierra Madre over a period of years. The hypothesis has its merits, for the Tehuacán valley was thoroughly irrigated by 900 B.C., unlike other areas of the New World, and Tehuacán peoples seem to have taken the skill with them wherever they went. The missionary-explorer Juan Nentvig wrote, "There is a tradition current among the Indians and Spaniards that the Mexicas, on their long transmigration, rested there." The Franciscan proselyte Pedro Font likewise observed more pointedly in 1775 that the three-story Casa Grande, or "Big House," at the Hohokam site of the same name owed its origins to a southerly people:

The large house or palace of Montezuma, according to the histories and meager accounts which we have from the Indians,

Casa Grande National Monument, near Coolidge, Arizona. The building stands three stories high. (Photograph by the author)

may have been built some five hundred years ago; for, as it appears, this building was erected by the Mexicans, when, during their transmigration, the Devil led them through various countries until they arrived at the promised land of Mexico; and in their sojourns, which were long, they formed towns and built edifices.

Font was strangely prescient, for the Casa Grande is indeed a twelfth- or thirteenth-century edifice that would astonish succeeding generations of Europeans who passed it. He was surely more prescient, in any event, than the nineteenth-century Anglo settler Oscar Hutton, who " 'llowed they mout 'a' been built by some o'them Egyptian niggers as built the pyramids in th' Bible."

But the Hohokam had been in the Gila valley for hundreds of

years before Casa Grande rose to greet the sky, and most modern archaeologists now believe that they were an already extant culture that received many technological and religious ideas, and perhaps a few migrants, from Mesoamerica. The early Hohokam were growing cotton near the site of present-day Phoenix at about A.D. 200–300, when many of their major cities, like Snaketown, were founded. At the peak of Hohokam civilization, their canals sustained a vast population of some sixty thousand or more, and from those canals grew a political system that the desert had not seen before.

Politics, it has been observed, is about the control of resources. In the 1950s a German scholar, Karl Wittfogel, developed a hypothesis that the tyrannical regimes of ancient Mesopotamia and China owed their origins to the rise of a political hierarchy directly related to the allotment of irrigation water, and it remains a compelling argument despite counterclaims that these societies, as well as the Hohokam, ceded irrigation districts to individual shareholders. In the case of the Hohokam, we have plenty of evidence of social stratification. They seem to have put their energies into large civic structures like ball courts, platform mounds, ceremonial complexes, and even pyramids, while their homes were in the main poorly made mud huts. All this suggests the existence of a ruling class not unlike the Mexican *cacique* of today. Such grand structures are not often voluntarily made, and likely an authoritarian force lay behind them.

Recent studies of Casas Grandes, Chihuahua, an ancient city just south of the Gila drainage, reinforce the idea of a Mesoamerican-style politics in the Southwest. Casas Grandes emerged as a major center at about A.D. 1300, and evolved an economy based on copper metallurgy and the breeding of macaws. Its buildings may have reached heights of five stories. Through this great center came the Mesoamerican masked-gods cult, which the late Hohokam and Anasazi cultures enthusiastically adopted, and which survives in the Puebloan katsina cult today. Charles DiPeso, who first excavated the site, believes that Casas Grandes was destroyed by contending warlords in about 1400, a period of cataclysmic change throughout the region.

The Hohokam were highly skilled stoneworkers, making ornaments and tools of malachite, azurite, chrysocolla, opal, chalcedony, and turquoise, all obtained from nearby mountains and the riverbed. They were equally adept at weaving cotton and agave fibers. (About the only neolithic technology the Hohokam, a peaceable people, seem not to have been particularly good at was the making of weaponry.) They traded these goods with traveling *pochtecas*, merchants from the Valley of Mexico, for exotic imports of macaws, copper bells, mosaic plaques, onyx bracelets, and pyrite mirrors.

The Hohokam also made seashells a major item of trade, and sought them avidly. They etched designs on particularly attractive specimens with an acid made of fermented saguaro juice, and surviving shells point to a high degree of artistry. They did not have far to look; the middle Gila teemed with freshwater clams until Coolidge Dam was completed in 1930. The hunting and gathering peoples of the western Papaguería, who made annual salt pilgrimages to the Gulf of California, also traded shells from the Gulf of California in exchange for the agricultural produce they lacked. These peoples collected their food from the native plants and animals of the desert, and dried corn and beans were a great boon when the rains failed to come.

By far the greatest Hohokam city was Snaketown, which lies on the banks of the Gila near the modern town of Casa Grande, Arizona. Founded at about A.D. 300, it sheltered thousands of Hohokam, who farmed the surrounding fields through a massive system of irrigation canals, raising two crops a year in March and August, when the river carried its greatest runoff from winter and summer rains. These canals were supplemented by wells, the Hohokam having discovered that alongside the river lay an abundant supply of groundwater.

An acid-etched seashell recovered from Snaketown, near Casa Grande, Arizona. (Photograph by Helga Teiwes, courtesy of the Arizona State Museum)

An aerial view of the ruins of Snaketown. The ruins are now closed to the public by order of the Akimel O'odham Tribal Council.
(Photograph by Helga Teiwes, courtesy of the Arizona State Museum)

Snaketown earned its name from the Pima Indians, who called it Skoakuik. The Hohokam, like many prehistoric peoples, were not particular about rubbish. Their cities were strewn with organic litter and broken pottery, and these garbage middens offered attractive nesting places for rodents, which in turn drew disproportionate numbers of predatory snakes. The Snaketown Hohokam seem not to have minded, and snakes are abundantly represented in their arts. In the 1870s, when a few Pima families moved to a site near Snaketown, large numbers of reptiles still congregated there to feed on the rodent cornucopia that existed long after the Hohokam had vanished. When I last walked along the river near the site I counted six rattlesnakes and many more king snakes and bull snakes in an area of a few acres.

In Snaketown and similar cities lay the seeds of the Hohokam's destruction. The sedentary urban populations grew, adding pressure to expand the agricultural base of the economy into ever more marginal areas farther and farther from flowing water. Much of the flow of the middle Gila and its nearby tributaries, the Salt and Agua Fria rivers, was diverted into irrigation canals, increasing the likelihood of periodic failures. In the ninth century, massive floods on the Gila and Salt destroyed hundreds of miles of Hohokam irrigation canals, causing a famine that may have lasted for a decade, and the rebuilding patterns suggest that Hohokam leaders decreed that they would not be caught shorthanded again.

Like Mesopotamia and the Maya Empire before it, Snaketown fell to salt. Desert rivers carry heavy concentrations of minerals and salts, and, as later generations of farmers would learn along with the Hohokam, irrigating fields with salty water is at best a temporary expedient. The salts remain on the surface of the ground, eventually forming a hard pan that neither digging stick nor plant root can easily break. Irrigating their crops twice a year with perhaps five feet of water per acre, the Hohokam fell victim to their own technological prowess;

*A modern Akimel O'odham farmer working an irrigated field near
the Pima Villages, following long-standing indigenous practices.*
(Photograph by Helga Teiwes, courtesy of the
Arizona State Museum)

one by one Hohokam fields drifted into ruin at a rate so gradual that
the farmers likely could not perceive the degradation until it was too
late to correct their methods.

At the same time, the Southwest endured a great drought that
lasted, with minor regional variations, from 1275 to 1350. The rains
refused to sweep inland from the sea, the snows did not fall, and the
once-full rivers became for a time the sandy, dead beds they are today.
In the face of drought and famine, the civilizations of the Southwest
imploded. The Anasazi abandoned their great cities of Mesa Verde
and Chaco Canyon; the Anasazi inhabitants of Betatakin quit the

pueblo so quickly that when it was discovered by a passing American rancher in 1907, Betatakin's apartments were full of baskets, pottery, and preserved grains and ears of corn, as if their occupants had been chased away in the middle of a meal. The Mogollon people of the Gila headwaters gradually left their cliff dwellings and pit houses and wandered away. And the great Hohokam metropolises became ghost towns, full of snakes and absent of the people whose name, in the language of the Tohono O'odham, means "all used up."

It was as if the population within the Gila's compass had simply disappeared into sand and rock.

The land is always stalking people.
The land makes people live right.
—ANNIE PEACHES, APACHE ELDER

3

MOUNTAIN PEOPLE, DESERT PEOPLE

The people of the Gila did not vanish. Instead, driven by the vicissi-
tudes of climate, they wandered in a great exodus from one corner of
the basin to another, eventually settling in a few hospitable pockets of
terrain, in canyon-shaded river bottoms and the handful of desert oases
that had somehow weathered the long drought.

Some of the Mogollon made their way north of the headwaters
and intermarried with refugee Anasazis; some archaeologists believe
them to be the ancestors of the Zuni. Others followed migratory game
animals and headed south into the highlands of the Sierra Madre,
where their culture evolved into the present-day Tarahumara. Still
other Mogollon wandered west, uniting with the easternmost Hohokam and a few Anasazi remnants to form a culture now known as the
Sobaípuri, centered on the junction of the Gila and San Pedro rivers.

Hohokam culture similarly splintered, but its people did not wander far from their ancestral lands. Their numbers were considerably

reduced, however. The riverine Hohokam, who evolved into the Akimel O'odham, "Running Water People," declined from perhaps a hundred thousand to some four thousand people. The desert Hohokam, who became the Tohono O'odham, "Stony Place People," never attained a population of more than six thousand, although their range comprised an area nearly the size of New England. These populations stood in rough balance with the carrying capacity of the drought-shorn desert; the land probably could have borne no more.

Both groups lost connection to their past. The Akimel O'odham forgot the Hohokam arts that had sustained their ancestral commodity culture, and their forebears soon came to be a great mystery to them. The art of etching shells with fermented saguaro juice was lost, for example, only to reappear in the 1970s, when Anglo anthropologists who were reconstructing Hohokam society taught Akimel O'odham artists how to make the necessary materials. But other lifeways continued: Akimel O'odham and Tohono O'odham basketry employed Hohokam motifs that were millennia old, most famously the "man in the maze." The Running Water People also eventually cleared out old irrigation canals that ran through places like Snaketown and Sacaton and resumed something of their former agricultural folkways, although they now depended on food gathered from the desert and river banks for more than half of their diet.

The Tohono O'odham, too, retained ancestral lifeways, among them the ceremony for which they are best known today. Early each June, from village to village, the Stony Place People are called together by the humming drone of a bullroarer—an instrument made of two slats of wood connected by a thong, resembling the nunchuks that martial artists employ—to drink wine made from the fruit of the saguaro cactus. They do this for two reasons: first, to honor the saguaro, *Cereus giganteus*, which they classify in the same semantic category as humans and protect by the same set of laws; and second, to encourage the arrival of the summer rainy season, which by long-standing tradition begins on June 24, the feast day of St. John the Baptist. (Nature rarely cooperates with the liturgical calendar. In the two decades I have lived in the Sonoran Desert, it has rained only twice on the twenty-fourth.)

An important element in this act is a repeated invocation for the clouds to appear, and with them the blessing of the water that they bear. Through sympathetic magic, Tohono O'odham adults emulate the clouds by glutting themselves with saguaro wine and then vomiting on the ground—much in the way a cloud picks up water from the air as it passes by, and then spits summer rain on the desert—while other adults and children sing rain songs. Tohono O'odham scholar and poet Ofelia Zepeda offers a translation of one:

> *And somewhere along the way I stopped again*
> *And it was my cloud that reached me*
> *And it was sprinkling wetly*
> *And here I reached your rainhouse and looked in*
> *There lay many winds, there lay many clouds,*
> > *there lay many seeded things*
> *And you set them down and sat upon them*
> *And with them I touched you*
> *And you moved and breathed your wind*
> *And with it were doing things*
> *Here you dropped it upon my land*
> *And with that my land was sprinkled*
> > *with water and was finished.*

The Tohono O'odham had reason to hope for an abundant rain and invested a great deal of cultural energy into song and ceremony to assure its coming, for in May and June they usually starved; their

An Akimel O'odham calendar stick. (Drawing by W. Eugene Hall)

name for the month of May remains *Ko'ok Mashat'*, "the Painful Time," when the last of the winter stores had been exhausted. Still, they enjoyed the diverse diet of the desert Hohokam, and had in their larder of acceptable foodstuffs the gray fox, kit fox, desert bighorn sheep, bats, pack rats, the boarlike javelina, antelope, rabbits, coyotes, skunks, ringtails, grasshoppers, wild turkeys, lizards, iguanas, snakes, beaver, frogs, and various kinds of deer. To these they added food from native plants like the blue paloverde (*Cercidium floridium*), which grows in abundance throughout the 119,000-square-mile Sonoran desert; the tornillo (*Prosopis pubescens*), a tree that grew to heights of thirty feet along the Gila, its sweet pods, like those of the mesquite (*Prosopis juliflora*) and ironwood (*Olneya tesota*), ground for a nutritious flour; the cholla (*Opuntia bigelovii*) and saguaro, which bear juicy, figlike fruits; and various varieties of agave, which provided fiber, food, and a range of impressive alcoholic beverages.

Along with the Akimel O'odham, the desert people made extensive use of the cottonwood (*Populus fremontii*) as well, using its soft, pliable wood as fuel and as material to make ceremonial drums and skirts, its ashes to manufacture dyes and mascaras. The O'odham developed an elaborate pharmacopoeia from other native plants, among them the desert paloverde (*Parkinsonia aculeata*), the bark of which was brewed to make a tea to treat fevers and epilepsy; desert gourds like the coyote gourd (*Cucurbita digitata*), a general tonic that, ethnobotanists have only recently discovered, can shrink tumors; and the tornillo, or screwpod mesquite, whose roots provided a soothing dress-

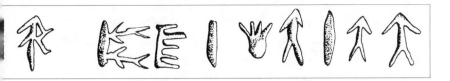

ing for wounds. This folk-medical knowledge, accumulated over the centuries, is today all but lost, given over to trips to the Indian Health Service and the local drugstore.

The traditional O'odham repertoire of foodstuffs and useful plants was more varied than that of contemporary Europeans. Still, the bounty did not impress the first Spanish to come to the Papaguería, one of whom called the desert dwellers "a poor people who lived by eating roots of wild sweet potatoes, honey, mesquite beans, and other fruits." He evidently kept his eyes closed to the rest of the O'odham larder, or he may have been writing of an offshoot group that lived near the Pinacate range in southwestern Arizona and northwestern Mexico, the so-called Papagos Areñeros or "Sand Papago." These lived chiefly on a sweet potato–like tuber called the sandroot (*Pholisma sonorae*), with a skin so tough that over time the historic Areñeros who ate it ground their teeth down to the gumline.

The Tohono O'odham were a "two-village" people. In the winter they lived in the foothills of the Basin and Range ridges that cut across the Papaguería, near permanent sources of water, while they moved in summer out on the plains, where they farmed along arroyos and at the deltas of the alluvial fans that spread down from the mountains. They grew a broad range of crops, including devil's claw, peppers, gourds, tobacco, maize, and their favorite, tepary beans. They were so fond of these beans that neighboring tribes called them by the Tohono O'odham name for the crop, *Bá bawi*, the source of the Spanish and Anglo approximation, "Papago."

In short, the O'odham, river and desert, adapted to the natural cycles of their environments, feasting in times of plenty, the majority of the year, and suffering in the month or two of acute scarcity. To call their existence idyllic is to impose Western standards on a people who might not have been able to translate such a term into their daily reality, and perhaps to romanticize them unduly, but it seems safe enough to say that "idyllic" is closer to the mark than Thomas Hobbes's conception of life in hunting and gathering societies as "nasty, brutish and short."

Indeed, anthropologist Marshall Sahlins has concluded that hunting and gathering peoples enjoy vastly more leisure time than do industrial peoples. For example, an African Bushman, working only four hours a day, can support five cohorts, and the native peoples of the Southwest very likely had even less work to do in gathering the abundance of their "desert," much richer in resources than the Kalahari. We have only to compare their regimen with our modern workweek, a division of life into wage work and "unproductive leisure" that began with the Industrial Revolution and Josiah Wedgwood's hellish pottery factories, where men and women who had hitherto set their own hours soon found themselves cast as "such machines of men as cannot err," putting in seventy-hour weeks in order merely to sustain themselves on the owners' pitiful wages.

The O'odham way of life had other advantages, too. Medical anthropology shows little evidence of major epidemics or nutritional stress in the prehistory of the Americas generally, and particularly the Southwest. The Mayan *Book of Chilam Balam* relates that "the Indians had no sickness; they had no aching bones; they had no burning chest; they had no abdominal pain; they had no consumption; they had no headache. At that time the course of humanity was orderly." Its author goes on to remark, "The foreigners made it otherwise when they arrived here." Given health and freedom, the occasional hunger must be accounted a relatively minor drawback.

Water lay at the heart of O'odham life, but it seems to have generated only a few organized rituals. Instead, water prohibitions found their expression in everyday beliefs, among them the notion that every water source had a serpent-god, a *corúa*, to watch over it. This water-snake connection is an ancient one, and its origins appear to be Mesoamerican; the Uto-Aztecan linguistic element *co* means "snake," and it turns up in the name of the Aztec plumed serpent-god of the east, Quetzalcoatl.

In O'odham belief these protector serpents were not aggressive, although they were endowed with huge fangs, and in any contact with humans *las corúas* usually lost. In the event of a serpent-god's death, the O'odham held, its associated spring would dry up, and perhaps the idea of such a vulnerable if fearsome-looking snake kept the desert people from tampering with precious watercourses. (The Mexican story of La Llorona, a weeping ghost who wanders along riverbeds and steals children who come too near, has a similar function.) Not all water serpents lived underground, however. Some dwelled in the hearts of the boiling summer thunderstorms that bring rain to the desert, not in life-replenishing droplets but in great black undulating curtains of water, leaving floods and destruction in their wake. It was no sin to kill such serpents, but even the most resourceful Tohono O'odham shaman was no match for the *corúas* of the air.

West of the Papaguería lay the territory of various Yuman-speaking tribes. Like the Tohono O'odham, the Cocopah and Quechan peoples, who lived along the lower Colorado near its confluence with the Gila, depended on floodwater irrigation to grow a few crops, of which the most important was panic grass (*Panicum sonorum*, or *simcha* in Yuman), a milletlike grain that grew on dried-up floodplains after they had been charged by the flood pulse. Apart from panic grass—which now is mostly grown from seedbank stock—and occasional patches of maize and agave, the Quechans relied on hunting and gathering for their daily sustenance. They also fished, using long spears to catch large quantities of trout (*Salmo gilae*) and squawfish (*Ptychocheilus lucius*) at the confluence of the Gila and Colorado.

Unlike their easterly neighbors, the Yumans were wholly given over to a complex ritualized warfare, which manifested itself in orchestrated raids on other riverine groups. The object of this warfare seems to have been various: to kill enemies, usually by bashing in their skulls with heavy war clubs; to seize women and thus enlarge the genetic stock of these none too populous groups; to gain new territories in special battles called "boundaries bristling side by side"; and, particularly, to gain the spiritual power that supposedly accrued to a successful killer. It may even have been a form of manly leisure. Yuman warfare was vicious and endemic enough that it caused large-scale migrations out of the Colorado River valley at about the time of the European arrival. Several tribes left the area and made their way to the more tranquil Pimería, among them the Kaveltcadom, Halchidoma, Kohuana, and Halyikwanai. On arriving at the Pima Villages along the fertile middle Gila, the refugees petitioned the Akimel O'odham for sanctuary and were granted leave to establish villages to the west of the Salt-Gila confluence. The Akimel O'odham, who had had their share of troubles with the Quechans, may have very well welcomed this creation of a buffer zone on the desert frontier.

They settled in, these Halchidoma, "people of the strange ways," as they now collectively called themselves. (Maricopa, the name by which they are now known, may be a transposition of the Spanish *mariposa*, "butterfly," for the way the Halchidoma painted their faces.) Their customs may indeed have seemed strange to their agriculturalist neighbors. Despite having access to the fertile bottom-

lands of the Gila—they called it *áxa*, which means simply "water"—
the Halchidoma did little farming. For the most part they hunted and
gathered, desert bighorn sheep (*Ovis canadensis*) and various kinds of
caterpillars and grubs being two staples of their diet, along with
roasted agave hearts. They developed a local trade in seashells, traveling to the Gulf of California to obtain them and trading their finds
with the Akimel O'odham for cornmeal and other foodstuffs. And,
unlike any other Southwestern people, the Halchidoma formally took
two months off every year: July, when it was too hot to travel, and
December, when it was too cold by their reckoning to go outdoors.

Theirs was a genteel poverty. The Halchidoma seem not to have
minded the relative lack of possessions, or even the occasional bout of
hunger, and they commemorated their simple way of life in their creation story. In it, the peoples of the earth gather to petition the creator
god for various favors and goods. The Chemehuevi people, the Halchidomas' former neighbors on the Colorado, talked long into the
night about trivial matters, for which reason the impatient creator
made their language unintelligible to anyone else. The Halchidoma
asked only for the occasional rain, the O'odham for saguaro fruits, and
the creator gladly obliged. A nineteenth-century addendum to the
story explains the ways of newcomers to the desert: "The white people
were the very last to speak. It was said, that like a younger child, they
were cry-babies. So the creator did everything to soothe them, hence
they are richer than any of the Indians."

Peace eventually came to the western Gila, marked by a large
mound of petroglyphs along the river near Gila Bend, Arizona. The
site of Painted Rocks State Park is believed to mark the boundary
between Halchidoma and Yuman territory, as a monument to a peace
treaty concluded some time in the early 1500s. John S. Griffin, a doctor who traveled along the Gila in 1848, was the first Anglo to describe
the mound:

Nov. 17th & 18th. One days march on the River is so much like unto another that one description will do for all that is to say— sand, dust, & black stone, so blistered from the effects of heat that they look like they had hardly got cool—no grass, nothing but weeds & cactus. The River here [near Dateland] is some 60 or 80 yards wide—on an average 3 feet deep and rapid. We have seen more water fowel in the last two days, than we have yet met with on the River—ducks, brant geese & swan. The cotton wood shows the effect of frost very little—not more than the same tree did when we left the Rio Grande a month since— On the night of the 17th we had considerable frost.—The moun- tains still continue on our right and left, and if any thing more jagged and forbidding in appearance than any we have yet passed. Some of them have the most fantastic forms. Our march for the last two days has been some 35 or 37 miles—I neglected to note a stone we passed on the 16th or rather a hill of stone— all carved up with Indian hieroglyphics—the sun moon & stars—horned frogs—Attempts at the human form divine, were the most frequent forms—they seemed to be of recent date— whether cut in sport or to commemorate some great event we could not tell.

The peace held for generations, broken every now and again by out- bursts of raiding along the river. The last instance of intertribal warfare occurred on September 1, 1857, when several hundred Quechan and Mojave soldiers attacked the Halchidoma settlement closest to the Pima villages after marching across nearly two hundred miles of desert, which the Halchidomas called "the land of the dead." The invaders were repulsed, and half of them were killed.

Quechan depredations would come to seem insignificant, however, compared to those visited upon the indigenes of the Gila by invaders from the north. Over a period of several centuries, these people, some five thousand of them, spread southward from an original culture area within the Mackenzie Basin of Canada, arriving in the Southwest sometime in the fifteenth century. They called themselves Diné, "the People," but they are better known as the Apache, a word that derives from the Zuni *apachù*, "enemy."

The Apache settled in the empty highlands along the headwaters of the Gila, branching out through tributary systems to control nearly the entire length of the Mogollon Rim and adjacent valleys. There they found an abundance of game and food plants, and in the green forests they must have thought they had found paradise, for in Apache cosmology the afterlife is divided into two distinct districts: a green, mountainous, pleasant place for the good, such as they now lived in; and a flat, barren, arid place for the bad, a place the Apaches may have thought fit only for farmers and desert wanderers like the O'odham.

Like most Native American groups, the Apaches were loosely anarchic, bound by clan rather than political ties, with a variable leadership made up of "chiefs" appointed for special purposes. They seldom made permanent settlements, and, viewing the stone ruins of the Mogollon peoples as the work of the *gan*, the mountain spirits who influence life for both good and ill, they shunned the places of their predecessors. Instead, they lived in easily movable wikieups— conical thatched huts made of mesquite or willow poles bound with agave fibers. They moved within unfixed territories, in which bands fanned out far enough away from others that the resources of any given area would not be overused. In time, separation would give these bands distinctive identities.

In the mountains and riverine canyons, the Diné found enough

*In the highlands of the Gila headwaters and the Mongollon Rim, the
Apaches made both their homes and their bases for raiding the
lowlands.* (Photograph by the author)

food to sustain themselves, and they farmed only occasionally until
recent times. Their diet was less catholic than that of the Mogollon
before them; the Apaches believed that owls, snakes, bears, and coyotes were beings into which dying sorcerers would inject their souls
so as to continue living, and hence were taboo. For mysterious reasons,
given the well-watered lands they now ruled and their northerly origins, the Diné also abstained from eating fish. Despite these restric-
tions, they had plenty of other options. Captain John Gregory Bourke,
a prescient student of their lifeways, recalled in his classic *On the Border
with Crook*, "The Apache was a hard foe to subdue, not because he
was full of wiles and tricks and experienced in all that pertains to the
arts of war, but because he had so few artificial wants and depended

almost absolutely upon what his great mother—Nature—stood ready
to supply."

Like many nomadic groups, the Diné looked down on farmers.
"Raids are our agriculture," a Saudi Bedouin once told the English
writer Bruce Chatwin. The sentiment might just as well have come
from the Apaches, who struck terror into the hearts of the O'odham
and Halchidoma with their frequent forays for grain and, on occasion,
blood. For doing so they acquired a reputation for cruelty, although
the myth-making machinery of dime novels and Hollywood westerns
has long exaggerated that fame.

In the highlands the Diné developed a complicated ecological
ethic, much of it apparently borrowed from the Hopi by way of the
Apaches' cousins, the Navajos, also a migrant newcomer to the region.
Among its fundamental tenets was the notion of "life in balance"
(*koyaanisqatsi*, in Hopi), an idea that social and personal health derived
from right living in one's chosen locale, resembling both the ancient
Indo-European humoral theory of health and illness and the Buddhist
precepts. Another was the idea of the seasonal nature of things: one
worked in the "dangerous times" of lightning, in the spring and fall,
and reserved the lightning-free times for attending to matters of the
soul, to telling stories and teaching the young. In all this the land itself
came to serve as moral arbiter, visiting its inhabitants with good luck
or bad depending on their actions. (I once heard of an Apache man
who boasted to an Anglo anthropologist of killing a herd of javelinas
for mere amusement. If the Diné are right, their kinsman is in for hard
times ahead.)

An early Spanish chronicler remarked of the highland Apaches,
"Water is what they worship most, to which they offer small painted
sticks and feathers and yellow powder made of flowers." Water ori-
ented the Apache universe. For example, Cibecue, a principal cere-

monial center, lies near a spring called *tú nchaa halíí* (literally, "much water flows up and out") that eventually debouches into the Salt River; from Cibecue have emerged many of the Diné's spiritual leaders. Such places were invested with magic and with unworldly protectors. The Apache tell a story about one of them, Tonto Natural Bridge along the East Verde tributary, made up of six billion cubic feet of travertine so hard that, fortunately, no way was ever found to mine it. In ancient times, the legend has it, a solid wall of stone formed the lower shore of a crystalline mountain lake in which a huge, guardian serpent dwelled. A great flood broke through the travertine embankment, leaving the arch in its wake, and the monster was washed down into the Salt River. Finding the lowland waters too warm and the local people too tame for its taste, the serpent made its way down the Gila and Colorado to the Gulf of California, where it presumably now dwells.

One can tell much about a people by its attitude toward the land. Looking into the hills above Whiteriver, Arizona, one elderly Apache remarked to anthropologist Keith Basso,

> *Even if we go far away from here to some big city, places around here keep stalking us. If you live wrong, you will hear the names and see the places in your mind. They keep on stalking you, even if you go across oceans. The names of all these places are good. They make you remember how to live right, so you want to re-place yourself again.*

Not long ago, a construction foreman ordered a group of Apaches on a work crew to cut down a stand of cottonwood trees in a floodplain along the upper Gila. When the foreman returned he found the workers lying under the trees they had been told to fell, smoking cigarettes and talking among themselves. When the foreman angrily asked why they had not followed his orders, one of the Apaches explained, "We can't cut down all the cottonwoods by this river. Something bad would happen to us."

They may have been thinking of an old Diné prophecy: "When the trees die, then the humans are next."

Men wearing clothes shall come,
dominate, and kill.
—Taino Prophecy

4

The First Conquest

Early in March of 1536 four wraithlike figures, dressed in tattered animal skins, stole out upon the coastal plain of Sonora, making their way seaward. On the outskirts of a small ranch they were hailed by a Spanish sentry, who demanded to know their identity. The leader spoke, and gladly. "Having almost despaired of finding Christians again," he later recalled, "we could hardly restrain our excitement."

On the first of April the four were led to the southerly provincial capital of Culiacán, where their leader told a fantastic story. His name, he related, was Alvar Núñez Cabeza de Vaca, the forty-four-year-old scion of landed gentry. His noble companions were Andres Dorantes de Carranza and Alonso de Castillo Maldonado, accompanied by Dorantes's Moorish servant, a manumitted slave called Estevánico. For more than two years they had been wandering on foot from the coast of Texas, where they had been shipwrecked with the ill-fated Narváez expedition in the winter of 1528. For six years they had remained on an island they had named Malhado, "Bad Luck," to commemorate the event, trading with the Karankawa Indians and passing the time as best they could. Finally, despairing of ever being rescued, their numbers thinned from some three hundred by disease, hunger, and Indian attacks to these remaining four, they waded to the mainland and set out on an overland journey far outside the compass of Spanish geography.

They saw and did miraculous things, Cabeza de Vaca reported. He himself had raised Indians, Lazarus-like, from the grave; had cured blindness and relieved illness; had preached the gospel of Jesus to countless nations, who honored him and his companions as gods. To be sure, they had had their share of hardships, crossing sun-blasted deserts for days without hope of finding water, enduring meals of mush made from tall grass and ground seeds, losing their youth to the rigors of aimless travel. They reported passing through towering mountains—which may well have been the Black Range, at the headwaters of the Gila River, and the Chiricahua Range to the southwest—and rolling grasslands, fording swollen rivers and traversing the territories of Indians friendly and hostile. One amicable band, who may have been Akimel O'odham at the Gila–San Pedro confluence, gave him, he said, "innumerable deerhide and cotton blankets, the latter better than those of New Spain, beads made of coral from the South Sea, fine turquoises from the north—in fact, everything they had, including a fine gift to me of five emerald arrowheads such as they use in their singing and dancing." Six hundred Indian acolytes had followed them, he continued, almost to the point where they first encountered other Spaniards.

His audience may have seen through Cabeza de Vaca's lies. He could not, after all, produce any of the treasures he claimed to have acquired. Their eyes widened nonetheless at another part of his account. The Indians to their north, he averred, had pointed the direction toward seven fabulous adjoining cities made entirely of gold. Their name, he said, was Cíbola.

As his story spread, Cabeza de Vaca was accused of sorcery and cannibalism, especially serious charges in those days of the Inquisition, one of the first Spanish institutions to be brought to the Americas; the inquisitors had recently meted two hundred lashes to a Mexico City cobbler who dared suggest that simple fornication was not a mortal sin. Cabeza de Vaca had an easier punishment, being simply deported to Spain. Not long after his arrival there he published a memoir called *Naufragios* (Shipwrecks), full of still more fantastic adventures. Appreciative readers in the court quickly rewarded his alleged exploits with an appointment as the royal captain-general of the Province of La Plata, comprising modern northern Argentina, Uruguay, and southern Paraguay. There he busied himself slaughtering Paraná and Guaycurú Indians and accumulating riches until he was deposed in 1544, exiled to Algeria, and finally allowed to return to Spain. He died nearly penniless in Seville in 1557.

Cabeza de Vaca may not have flourished in the New World, but his tale of Cíbola did. Three years after Cabeza de Vaca's arrival, Francisco Vasquez de Coronado, the governor of the province of Nueva Galicia, dispatched Estevánico and Friar Marcos de Niza to the northern frontier of New Spain with orders to locate the cities of gold. De Niza returned several months later with mixed reports: they had found the cities, he proclaimed, but hostile Indians had murdered Estevánico. (It turned out that Estevánico had developed a taste for lording it over the aborigines he encountered. After he bedded, beat, and killed several Zuni women, the men of the pueblo hacked him to bits.) De Niza sketched out a journey of several thousands of miles, recounting, like Cabeza de Vaca, great mountains and rivers and uncounted riches. Rodrigo de Albornóz, the royal treasurer of New Spain, summarized de Niza's report:

*There are seven very populous cities with great buildings. . . .
The name of one where he has been is Cíbola, the others are in
the Kingdom of Marata. There is very good news of other very
populous countries, of their riches and good order and manner
of living, also of their edifices and other things. They have houses
built of stone and lime, being of three stories, and with great
quantities of turquoise embedded in the doors and windows. Of
animals there are camels and elephants and cattle . . . and a
great number of sheep like those of Peru, also other animals with
a single horn reaching to the ground, for which reason they must
feed sideways. These are not unicorns but some other kind of
creature. The people are said to go clothed to the neck, like Moors.
They are known to be people of solid understanding.*

On February 22, 1540, Coronado set out from his capital of Com-
postéla with three hundred Spanish soldiers and a retinue of more than
a thousand Mexican Indian bearers. They trudged northward through
Sonora, eventually crossing rough mountain country that left his men
and animals exhausted. But when they left the mountains, he recalled,
"we found fresh rivers and grass like that of Castille." Scholars argue
over his route, but he was probably describing the Gila valley in the
vicinity of present-day Safford, Arizona, near the now-lost ruins of a
pueblo he called Chichilticalli, "the Red House."

The territory, Coronado reported, was *despoblada*, "uninhabited."
Since the decline of the Hohokam and Mogollon civilizations, the
human population of the Gila basin had indeed fallen. But Coronado
had a vanguard unknown to him: disease. Successive epidemics of viral
sickness introduced from Europe to Mexico, including smallpox, probably reached the upper Gila by 1520, twenty years before Coronado's
entrada. Certainly there is evidence of widespread depopulation
throughout the Americas during that period: Coronado's description

of the area as *despoblada* and the abandoned "red house" are mute witnesses. By 1600 the native population of parts of the continent had fallen by as much as 80 percent, laid low by smallpox, measles, influenza, typhus, pertussis, bubonic plague, tuberculosis, diphtheria, mumps, and yellow fever. In central Mexico, the Indian population declined from 7.5 million in 1520 to 1.4 million by 1610; throughout New Spain as a whole, there were 25 million Indians in 1519, and only 1 million a century later.

Helpless in the face of such lethal diseases, which the Akimel O'odham called "wandering sicknesses," the indigenes could assume only that they had upset the dieties, and their first reaction was to burn suspected witches in order to appease their aggrieved gods. In later years, when the most virulent disease had been named, they would declare, "I like Smallpox," in the hope that smallpox would return the compliment and leave them alone. They had another explanation, too: children, who usually sickened and died first, were thought to have impeded the progress of desert tortoises by turning them upside down, and the tortoises' guardian spirits, more aggressive than *corúas*, were exacting brutal vengeance.

Coronado's force likely crossed the Gila at its confluence with the San Pedro, followed Cherry Creek northward into Apache country, and topped the Mogollon Rim in the vicinity of the present town of Show Low, Arizona. Strangely, they encountered no Indians, although Diné scouts must surely have trailed them. From there they pressed on to the northeast, following de Niza's roughly outlined map, until they encountered a dusty mesatop village called Shiwona, or Zuni, a word Spanish ears heard as "Cíbola."

It was not made of gold. It was instead, Coronado reported, "a small rocky pueblo, all crumpled up, there being many farm settlements in New Spain that look better from afar." The inhabitants, whom Coronado had to battle into surrendering on July 7, 1540, seemed to have had no knowledge of precious metals, nor much interest in the Spaniards' lust for riches. Infuriated, Coronado wrote to the ruler of New Spain, Viceroy Mendoza, that Friar de Niza "has not told the truth in a single thing he has said, for everything is the very opposite of what he related except the name of the cities." Wounded in the siege of Zuni, Coronado spent the rest of the summer resting and, when the spirit moved him, conquering neighboring pueblos, first reading aloud a document called the *Requerimiento*, which demanded of the Indians devotion to the Catholic church, the pope, and the king and queen of Spain; and then leading his men into battle against the unfortunate Indians with the war cry *¡Santiago y a ellos!* "In the name of Saint James, at them," used for centuries in the holy war against the Moors.

The disappointed Coronado led his force onto the Plains of San Agustín down to the Río Grande, where a Tigua Indian told him of a great city far to the east called Quivira. Still bent on chasing down the chimera, Coronado determined that this must be Cíbola, and for the next two years he and his force trod the Great Plains as far east as Kansas near the Iowa border. The Indian settlements he found were, like Zuni, innocent of gold. After taking a bad fall from his horse, Coronado turned his men—now a mere handful, thanks to war and the rigors of the trek—southwestward and plodded back to Mexico by way of the southern Gila basin, where one of his soldiers recalled seeing so many bison that he "did not know what to compare them with except the fish in the sea."

The quest for gold ruined Coronado, as it would so many other conquistadores. A startled contemporary, Lorenzo de Tejada, a jurist with the Audiencia, wrote to the Spanish emperor: "Francisco Vasquez came to his home, and he is more able to be governed in it than to govern outside it. He is lacking in many of his former fine qualities and he is not the same man he was when your Majesty appointed him to governorship." He retained his post as governor of Nueva Galicia for only another two years. His health steadily declined, and Francisco Vasquez de Coronado died on his ranch outside Mexico City on September 22, 1554, at the age of forty-four.

In the next four decades the Spanish staged various military reconnaissances into the Gila basin—brief forays meant only to determine "the situation of the nations" there. In the main the conquistadores, most of them from the arid Spanish provinces of Andalusia and Estremadura, were pleased by the country they saw. Certainly it was richer than the land they had left behind them, for Spain was by the fifteenth century a desertified land, a high plateau ringed by mountains that permitted little rain to cross by way of the ocean winds. Deforested in Roman times—the timber used to build Columbus's three caravels had to be imported from Norway—the porous limestone soils of Spain never recovered their ability to retain stores of surface water, and goats, voracious creatures, had browsed most of the remnant vegetation, leaving the country a near wasteland.

Long poor in natural resources, the Spanish had eagerly jumped into the business of international conquest. Their first ventures in the Spice Islands, and later the Americas, revolutionized the European economy, yielding such innovations as investment financiers, a banking system based on credit and growth, and what is now called "free enterprise." Those ventures, eminently practical, were fueled by a myth that Cabeza de Vaca would later make much of: the Iberian explorers hoped to make contact with the Christian potentate Prester John, whose fabulously wealthy kingdom was rumored to lie somewhere in the highlands of the Indies. The search for this mythical Prester John would sustain Spanish exploration along the Pacific Coast and the rivers of the West as surely as the promise of Cíbola kept Coronado's men at their quest, and it helped drive the later Spanish search for the Northwest Passage.

The Spanish had found in the Americas a granary that would become the breadbasket of empire, and all that remained was to bring Spain to the new lands. The Spanish conquistadores used the Antilles as a breeding ground for European animals that were to be introduced to subsequently conquered mainland territories, the first example of "ecological imperialism" in the Americas. Foremost among these animals was the churro sheep, a voracious variety developed by Roman breeders who grazed them in North Africa until the once-rich coastal grasslands were shorn to the ground; to these were later added the equally hungry merino sheep, the breeding of which was a peninsular royal monopoly until the 1600s, when the Spanish soil could no longer support grazing herbivores in numbers. Another animal was the fleet Spanish horse, the progenitor of several American breeds. First brought to the Antilles by Columbus on his second voyage, horses were introduced en masse to Mexico by Viceroy Antonio de Mendoza, and by 1560 hundreds of thousands of them grazed in massive herds on the grasslands of Sonora and the Pimería Alta, as the Spanish called the O'odham heartland.

Still, these would cause relatively little damage compared with another Spanish import: cattle. In the late 1520s there were perhaps half a million cattle scattered throughout Mexico, a number that had swelled to eight million a century later, in direct inverse proportion to the Indian population. In 1598, having successfully petitioned the Spanish crown for governorship of the new province of New Mexico, the conquistador Juan de Oñate y Salazar drove seven thousand head of cattle and as many churro sheep into the Gila drainage, where the native tall grasses, he reported, stood as high as a man on horseback. Oñate had earlier explored the lower reaches of the Colorado, where a Quechan recounted tales of a desert people who lived along the Gila and who had ears so large that they could shelter half a dozen normal people from the fierce heat. Another nation, he said, slept the night through under water, while yet another slept in trees, and yet another had only one foot. Less gullible than Coronado, Oñate continued his reconnaissance, made his maps, and returned to Mexico City content in the belief that he had seen what was important to see.

Oñate established his capital in Santa Fe, from which he scattered settlements along the Río Grande. He had little trouble finding willing settlers, for former conquistadores were granted estates called *encomiendas* that increased in size as they approached the northern frontier of New Spain. Within a dozen years these estates boasted hundreds of thousands of cattle; a French visitor remarked on "the great level plains, stretching endlessly and covered with an infinite number" of them. To support the vast ranches, Oñate ordered the native Puebloan peoples to pay tribute in the form of corn and cotton blankets, a great hardship. Other Indians were simply drafted to live on the ranches in exchange for board, a form of indenture that directly violated the so-called New Laws of 1542, written after Pope Paul III had declared in his papal bull of 1537, *Sublimis Deus*, that Indians had souls and could therefore not be kept as chattel.

Practice did not follow theory, as the Spanish friar Bartolomé de las Casas noted in 1543, decrying those of his countrymen who "for greed turn Jesus Christ into the cruelest of gods and the king into a wolf ravening for human flesh." Slavery technically did not exist, but this was a mere legal nicety. In its place came the *repartimiento*, where Indians who lived on or near Spanish settlements were allotted to Spanish employers, as fieldhands or cowherds or, increasingly, as miners; especially compliant indigenes were rewarded with posts as *gobernadores* (mayors) and *mayordomos* (irrigation bosses). The *rancherías* that sprang up downslope of the Gila headwaters were largely staffed by Pueblo Indians from northern New Mexico, for the local Apaches could not be induced to come down from their mountain strongholds and surrender their freedom to these more recent invaders. When they left the highlands at all, it was to steal Spanish cattle and horses, the second of which would soon lend them yet another tactical advantage. Apache raids kept the Spanish settlers confined to the lowlands, despite well-organized campaigns led by estimable soldiers like Don Juan Ignacio Flores de Mogollón, for whom the Mogollon Rim is named. Those raids also cost the Spanish dearly; Padre Morfi of El Paso counted ten thousand *mesteños*, or mustangs, at the headwaters of the Gila in 1777.

The Apaches would not be the sole enemy. The Pueblos, generally peaceable, tolerated Spanish rule for nearly a century. In 1680, however, tired of the demands of the *hidalgo* dandies and brown-robed priests who lorded it over them, the Río Grande pueblos exploded in revolt. The entire Spanish population of New Mexico was massacred or driven out, and for the next twelve years—until the province was reconquered pueblo by pueblo—New Mexico was free of European rule.

For the first two centuries of their tenure in New Spain, the Spanish kept clear of the deserts—infernal regions that seemed to them best suited to Moors and devils. Alarmed by French incursions into the northern Great Plains, however, the Crown determined to extend its military influence northward. The chief vehicle was not to be strictly martial. One of Spain's great soldiers was a Jesuit priest, Eusebio Francisco Kino, who came to the Pimería Alta in 1687.

An Italian from the Tyrol, an ascetic who used neither salt nor spices, wore sackcloth, and slept on a horse blanket, Kino was known for both his footlooseness and his cruelty. He could not stay put, and during his twenty-five years in Sonora, he made more than fifty trips inland, at distances of one hundred to a thousand miles each, mapping for the first time the lower reaches of the Gila and establishing the course of El Camino del Diablo, "the devil's highway," a stark stretch of desert that lies along the present boundary of western Arizona and

An artist's rendering of Father Eusebio Francisco Kino. (Courtesy of the Arizona Historical Society)

northwestern Sonora, Mexico. His harshness was another matter: among the Indians of the Pimería Alta he was renowned for his quickness with the lash, by which Kino presumed to improve their reception of the divine message he had been charged with delivering.

Apart from spreading the gospel, Kino's chief duty was to establish missions, each a combination of church, ranch, and fortress, from northern Sonora to the Gila River. He founded several, the northernmost of which lay a hundred miles south of the Gila along the Río Santa Cruz, a small tributary stream. To populate these missions, Kino refined a policy called *reducción*, "reduction," where the Indians who hitherto had dispersed themselves across the desert were rounded up into villages, similar to the "hamletization" policy of the U.S. government in Vietnam. The idea was to keep an eye on the nevertrustworthy (in Spanish eyes) indigenes while having a large pool of labor on which to draw.

The *reducción* policy had far-reaching effects. The O'odham had lived in small groups across a vast landscape for good reason: it prevented them from overtaxing the resources of the desert, from gathering wild foods to the point of depleting a given territory. Now herded into small areas, the O'odham exhausted native foodstuffs that lay within easy distance of the missions, and one by one their usual victuals, from devil's claw to mesquite pods, gave way to the wheat breads, beef dishes, and refined sugars of the conquerors. The change in diet caused a marked rise in diabetes, still prevalent today; genetically, the O'odham have few active insulin receptors, a trait that once enabled the O'odham to live on sugars stored in their bloodstream during times of famine. *Reducción* also made the O'odham easy prey for diseases like typhus, smallpox, and syphilis, the most powerful weapons in the Spanish arsenal; for pulmonary diseases caused by soil bacilli turned up by the Spaniards' deep plow, the *arado dental*, in nearby fields; and for aquatic diseases like yellow fever and malaria, carried by mosquitoes that had traveled in the bilges of the first caravels and that depended on standing water such as the newly dug Spanish wells and shallow irrigation canals provided. The *reducción* program, intentionally or not, penned the Indians like animals, while much of the surrounding desert lay unpeopled and ungathered.

The O'odham occasionally resisted this forced conversion to Christianity and settled life, for they regarded the Spanish reliance on force as inhuman and had heard from neighboring tribes to the south that the Spanish cattle caused watering holes to go dry. When they did resist, a mission or two fell to flames, a priest or two to a knife or war club, like Guevavi mission and its warden, Johannes Grazhofer. One noteworthy rebellion came in 1756, when a Halchidoma who lived among the Pima, Háwan Mo'o, raised a guerrilla band that nearly succeeded in driving the Spanish from the Pimería Alta.

More than any other missionary-soldier in the Gila basin, Kino reshaped the landscape of the desert. He was doubtless mindful of the Biblical authority Genesis 1:23 invested in his work: "and God said unto them, Be fruitful, and multiply, and replenish the earth, and subdue it; and have dominion over the fish of the sea, and over the fowl of the air, and over every living thing that moveth upon the earth." In that spirit, Kino sponsored numerous public-works projects, especially for agricultural irrigation, and created a new economy in the lands under his charge, an economy based on apiculture, horse breeding, and cattle ranching, with tallow, meat, and hides sold for export to sustain the northern missions. (Small wonder that a chief feature of Indian uprisings was the mass slaughter of mission livestock.) His "improvements" may have fallen afoul of the directives of the church, which had decreed a century earlier that "he sins against Divine Providence who tries to improve what God, for inscrutable motives, has wished to leave imperfect," but Kino had his answer in the Spanish law of the Sieta Partidas, enacted in 1265, which underlay the colonial

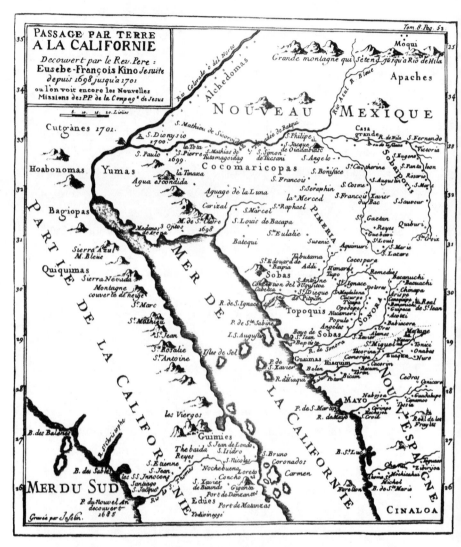

Father Kino's map of the Papaguería. The Gila is identified as the "R. de Hila." (Courtesy of the Donald B. Sayner Collection)

laws of the Americas: "Man has the power to do as he sees fit with those things that belong to him according to the laws of God and man."

Qui multum peregrinatur, raro sanctificatur, the Latin tag has it: "who travels much is rarely made a saint." Eusebio Francisco Kino traveled the length of the middle and lower Gila a dozen times, extending the "rim of Christendom" almost to its banks. He was careful to record what he saw along his travels, and his notes provide us with an index of what has been lost since his time. Of the Maricopa nation of the middle river, which he called the Río de los Apostoles, he remarked, "All its inhabitants are fishermen. . . . In some places they gave us so much and so very good fish that we gave it as a ration to the men, just as beef is given where it is plentiful."

Kino, too, sought Cíbola. He came closest to it when his military attaché, Lieutenant Juan Mateo Manje, reported that while surveying the lower Gila he had come across an Indian streaked with red hematite—quicksilver, said Kino's contemporary Father Bernal, citing Agricola's *De Re Metallica* as his authority. Kino urged that Spanish mining engineers and Indian conscript laborers be sent at once to the western desert, for quicksilver was a royal monopoly and Kino's missions could thereby become the richest in the Americas. (The Indian, Manje reported, told him that white men and women had recently visited his people. This gave Kino fits, for he assumed that the Indian could be referring only to the ever-encroaching French.) The viceroy ignored Kino's recommendation, and because of the Apaches' martial skills, Spanish settlement never extended farther north than the presidio of Tucson, ninety miles south of the great river.

Lying alongside the Santa Cruz tributary, the presidio was founded in 1775 by Don Hugo Oconor, born Hugh O'Conor, an Irish rebel in the service of the Catholic king of Spain. The presidio was moved from Tubac, forty miles to the south, because it was closer to the Gila and thus to the Apachería, but it scarcely mattered; emboldened by the Europeans' apparent lack of military ability, the Apaches had taken to raiding far deep into Mexico, burning the city of Mazatlán to the ground and besieging the city of Durango, far outside their usual territory. They also attacked Tucson with a frequency that must have appalled Oconor. Terrenate, another presidio that lay on the San Pedro tributary near the present town of Tombstone, Arizona, held out against Apache depredations for only five years. With its demise the Spanish "reduced" the Sobaípuri people, the last of the western Mogollons, removing them from the San Pedro Valley and resettling them among the Akimel O'odham along the Gila.

Unable to conquer the Apachería, the Spanish resorted to both holding actions and war by proxy, recruiting O'odham and Maricopa mercenaries to fight their battles. The Spanish introduced a novel method of taking body count: for every ear brought in they paid twenty pesos, for every scalp fifty. (There was no way to determine, of course, whether these were truly of Apache provenance.) By 1800, when the route south from the newly discovered Santa Rita copper mines at the Gila's headwaters fell under constant Apache attack, the rate increased to a hundred pesos for each head of enemy hair. Soon a mat of scalps numbering in the thousands bedecked the great doors of the cathedral in Chihuahua City.

Ignaz Pfefferkorn, a German Jesuit posted to the Pimería in 1756, relates that a Mimbres Apache who wanted to become a Christian convinced his people to stop warring against the Spanish. A Spanish captain rewarded him by ambushing his band and taking him prisoner; he planned to lead the Mimbres man in chains to Mexico City as a trophy of the war against the Apaches. The Mimbreño managed somehow to escape, and he went back to the mountains with a renewed hatred of the conquerors. By the captain's act the Spanish lost any hope of gaining the territory north of the Gila, and the river forever

The Santa Rita del Cobre mines as they appear today. (Photograph by the author)

marked the no-man's-land that separated them from the great riches the mountains held.

Pfefferkorn may have sympathized somewhat with the Apaches, but the peaceful agriculturalists under his charge were another matter:

> *Their natural stupidity, their complete neglect of themselves, the baseness of their spirits; these are the main sources of the hardness of their minds and, as it were, of their insensitivity. Would that the indifference with which they view everything transitory did not extend to the eternal and to the care of their souls.*

The farmers took small revenge by serving Pfefferkorn a bowl of chile-laden meat as his first meal in the Pimería, which he remembered years later in his memoir *Sonora: A Description of the Province*: "The constant use of this hot sauce is at first an unbelievable hardship for the Europeans. . . . After the first mouthful the tears started to come. I could not say a word and believed I had hellfire in my mouth."

Pfefferkorn's book, a mix of straightforward description and religious prescription, provides a remarkable account of the Pimería after two hundred years of Spanish rule. He did not enjoy his posting, it is clear, but he was as careful as Kino to record what he experienced:

Since the heat in May, June, and July is already so intense, it would necessarily be quite unbearable during the hot season in August and September were the heat not moderated, in Sonora as in New Spain in general, by daily rains. Consequently, this season is called tiempo de aguas, *or the rainy period. It begins in July and ends in September. The rain is not continuous, but passes off in two or three hours. However, the precipitation is so heavy that brooks and rivers are extraordinarily swollen and are very dangerous to those who, because of pressing need or audacity, would cross them on horseback, for there are no bridges in this country. When the storm has ended, the rivers fall again as rapidly as they have risen, and the sky assumes its former brightness. These rain showers are not general; at times they affect a stretch of but a few miles, over which the rain-cloud empties itself, while the surrounding regions remain completely dry. Where rain does not occur for some days, field products, especially maize or Indian corn, stand in danger of drying up, because it is not everywhere possible to irrigate the country from ditches. However, such a misfortune is not very often to be feared. After the first heavy shower the heat is indescribable, so that at night as well as in the daytime one nearly suffocates. After some days, though, the air becomes cooled by repeated rains and the heat so moderated that it is quite bearable.*

Sonora, through these daily rains, receives a pleasant relief from the heat, and at the same time its products are increased. Hence, these rains would surely be considered as priceless blessings of nature were they not always accompanied by the most horrible thunder-storms, which not infrequently do great damage to men and animals in the villages and in the fields. One cannot listen to the continuous crashing of the thunder without shuddering. At times such thunder-storms bring with them a damaging hail, which destroys all growing things in the field and garden; or there may occur a ruinous cloudburst, in Sonora called culebra de agua, *or water snake, which will flood over country and villages, devastating them. Sometimes the thunder-storms are accompanied by violent windstorms and whirlwinds, which lift the sand in a very thick, twisted column almost to the clouds. Nothing these whirlwinds seize can withstand their power. Even the strongest trees are often uprooted, roofs are uncovered, and houses upset, if they are not very solid.*

Pfefferkorn found the desert surpassingly strange, and especially the animals that populated it. One of the strangest was the Gila monster (*Heloderma suspectum*), the beaded, venomous lizard that unfortunately has many of the characteristics of the basilisk, that fantastic creature of the medieval Catholic bestiary "which frequents desert places and before people can get to the river it gives them hydrophobia and makes them mad. . . . It can kill with its noise and burn people up, as it were, before it decides to bite them." Now, Gila monsters are timid, small-jawed creatures, and a human has to work to get one to land a bite; still, countless numbers of the reptiles ended up skewered on Spanish lances in an effort to purify the Crown's holdings. The same fate befell rattlesnakes, "the most villainous kind of beast"; mountain lions, whose "only enemy is the dragon"; tarantulas, harmless spiders whose name derives from a pagan cult in post-Christian Taranto, Italy; wolves and bears; and innumerable other creatures.

In 1767 the Spanish king expelled the Jesuits from Spain and all its holdings, jealous of the order's powers and suspecting it of plotting against him. Franciscan priests took the Jesuits' place, gray robes replacing black ones, and they continued the work of bringing the Pimería Alta firmly under Spanish rule. One missionary-soldier, Francisco Garcés, courageously explored most of what is now Arizona and western New Mexico, providing the most accurate geographical survey of the time, and was rewarded with a curate at the confluence of the Gila and Colorado rivers. There he ordered his Quechan charges to plow up fields of panic grass and replace the native crop with a Spanish garden, including wheat that he brought from Mexico and that soon was "so well sprouted that the best irrigated wheat in our country does not equal it," black-eyed peas, watermelons, and muskmelons, all for export to settlements on the Gulf of California. Closest to Garcés's heart was black mustard, the seed Jesus likened to the kingdom of heaven, which the Quechans grew in commercial quantities and sold throughout Mexico and California. Alas for Garcés, his was not to be the Garden of Eden. A group of Quechans clubbed him to death as he said Mass in June 1781, repaying him for the cruelties he had visited upon them for the last five years. The provincial governor of New Spain sent a punitive expedition the next year to avenge Garcés's death, and Spanish soldiers killed some two hundred Indians and took a like number as slaves for the silver mines of Potosí. Still, with Garcés's murder Spain lost its grip on the lower Colorado once and for all.

Spain's days were waning in any event. It had squandered its vast wealth, taken from the fields and mines of the New World, in a century of wars against the forces of the Counterreformation; the lands of Spain were exhausted, and periodic famines swept the country; and independence movements at the beginning of the nineteenth century whittled away Spain's New World empire bit by bit. Mexico achieved independence in 1821, and Spanish forces withdrew from the northern provinces, never to be replaced. Their legacy was a chain of broken, weather-beaten missions; thousands of abandoned, now feral cattle and horses; a mestizo population that numbered no more than two thousand across the entire Gila drainage; and a handful of place names that would soon be all but lost to European memory.

It appeared that the Pimería would be the province of a new empire, whose language of power would be Diné.

Barbarism torments the body;
civilization torments the soul.
—COL. RICHARD I. DODGE

5

GATHERING
STORMS

In the early fall of 1824 a party of American trappers followed the
Santa Fe Trail from Council Bluffs, Iowa, to its terminus in New
Mexico. They were the first Anglos to have approached the capital in
eighteen years, since Lieutenant Zebulon Pike, surveying the new
lands of the Louisiana Purchase, had been jailed there in 1806 on the
entirely reasonable charge of espionage. (The mayor soon released
him with the proviso that Pike get out of Spanish territory at once.
Pike did.) On arriving in Santa Fe the Americans met with the Mexican governor, who granted them a license to trap beaver along the
Gila River. The drainage was still largely unknown, and the governor
reasoned that he might be able to attain a more or less accurate geographical survey of the region at the cost of a few pelts to the Mexican treasury.

Among the party's number was young James Ohio Pattie, the son
of its leader, Sylvester Pattie, and probably the first United States cit-

izen to see the Colorado Delta and the Grand Canyon. James Ohio Pattie had a keen eye for the details of the landscape if an overly heightened sense of exaggeration, and his *Personal Narrative*, ghost-written by newspaper editor Timothy Flint of Cincinnati and first published in 1831, remains an indispensable source of information on the Gila basin.

For nearly two years the party traveled the length of the river, which James Ohio Pattie called the Helay, killing thousands of beaver and a few hundred Indians, ranging as far south as Baja California and as far north as the Mojave Desert of California. They endured great hardships along the way, relying on an unpredictable diet of game while ignoring the abundant food plants around them, and they had a talent for choosing the most tortuous routes the river could offer. One such path brought them through the transition zone from the upper to the middle Gila, where the watercourse leaves the mountains of New Mexico and enters what is now Arizona:

On the morning of the 13th [of December, 1824] we started early, and crossed the river, here a beautiful clear stream about thirty yards in width, running over a rocky bottom, and filled with fish. We made but little advance this day, as bluffs came in so close to the river, as to compel us to cross it thirty-six times. We were obliged to scramble along under the cliffs, sometimes upon our hands and knees, through a thick tangle of grape-vines and under-brush. Added to the unpleasantness of this mode of getting along in itself, we did not know, but the next moment would bring us face to face with a bear, which might accost us suddenly. We were rejoiced, when this rough ground gave place again to the level bottom. At night we reached a point, where the river forked, and encamped on the point between the forks. We found here a boiling spring so near the main stream, that the fish caught in one might be thrown into the other without leaving the spot, where it was taken. In six minutes it would be thoroughly cooked. . . .

On the 20th we came to a point, where the river entered a cavern between two mountains. We were compelled to return upon our steps, until we found a low gap in the mountains. We were three day's crossing, and the travelling was both fatiguing and difficult. We found nothing to kill.

On the 23rd we came upon the river, where it emptied into a beautiful plain. We set our traps, but to no purpose, for the beavers were all caught, or alarmed. The river here pursues a west course. We travelled slowly, using every effort to kill something to eat, but without success.

On the morning of the 26th we concluded, that we must kill a horse, as we had eaten nothing for four day's and a half, except the small portion of a hare caught by my dogs, which fell to the lot of each of a party of seven. Before we obtained this, we had become weak in body and mind, complaining, and desponding of our success in search of beaver. Desirous of returning to some settlement, my father encouraged our party to eat some of the horses, and pursue our journey. We were all reluctant to partake of the horse-flesh; and the actual thing without bread or salt was as bad as the anticipation of it. We were somewhat strengthened, however, and hastened on, while our supply lasted, in the hope of either overtaking those in advance of us, or finding another stream yet undiscovered by trappers.

The latter desire was gratified the first of January, 1825. The stream, we discovered, carried as much water as the Helay, heading north. We called it the river St. Francisco. After travelling up its banks about four miles, we encamped, and set all our traps, and killed a couple of fat turkies. In the morning we examined our traps, and found in them 37 beavers! This success restored our spirits instantaneously. Exhilarating prospects now opened before us, and we pushed on with animation.

They were indeed animated. Within the next two weeks, Pattie records, the party killed some thousand beavers, which seemed to be an inexhaustible resource. The trappers stood to earn six dollars for each pelt, a huge sum at the time, easily the equivalent of two hundred dollars today. Their zeal soon resulted in significant damage to the population; Pattie noted that the number of beaver had mysteriously fallen, and with that decline seven discontented trappers had deserted the party to strike out on their own. The larger party later found the head of one deserter alongside the Gila, stuck on a stake and pincushioned with the arrows of Apache marksmen, who had taken care to replace the gentleman's leather hat on his head before they left.

The dispirited expedition returned to the Santa Rita copper mines at the headwaters of the Gila, far less wealthy than they had hoped. There James Ohio Pattie joined another trapping party organized by the Robidoux brothers of St. Louis. He never found his fortune, and he eventually returned to his native Kentucky, where he is thought to have died during the great cholera epidemic of 1833 at the age of twenty-nine.

More than any other economic activity, the fur trade opened the West to American expansion. The way had long been prepared by French explorers who had been mapping the mountain West at the time the Spanish were founding the first presidios. The French were driven by powerful currents of trade: in 1638 Charles II of England had mandated the wearing of beaver hats by all but the poor, and other fashion-conscious monarchs quickly followed his lead. Felt making became a major industry throughout Europe, but the European beaver had been driven into extinction by 1600, and new sources of fur were required. This economic vacuum occasioned the simultaneous opening both of the American hinterland and of Siberia, and for the next two and a half centuries a great flood of beaver pelts poured from east and west into the great fur centers of Inverness, Amsterdam, Cherbourg, Stockholm, and London.

The American trappers are engraved in the history of the West—men like Bill Williams, Cérain St Vrain, Charles Bent, and Kit Carson. None were as heroic as textbooks and roadside markers make them out to be; some were downright psychopathic, some comparatively gentle. They came from a variety of backgrounds. Antoine Leroux, for example, was the son of French St. Louis's leading family, an intellectual who had been educated at the Sorbonne and knew ancient Greek lyric poetry as well as he did the deployment of springjaw traps. Another trapper, Bill Williams, now memorialized as "Old Bill" but called "Crazy Bill" by his contemporaries, was born in Rutherford County, North Carolina, in 1787. He went west as an itinerant Baptist preacher, but he soon traded in the Bible for a rifle and bottle. "He was even readier to take a scalp than an Apache," one of his contemporaries observed (the Apaches had taken up this Spanish inventory-keeping system with a vengeance), and Williams himself admitted that "all of us continued to kill every Apache we could get the drop on. We were not so very particular whether he was an Apache, but he was killed anyway." Another trapper, a footloose Scots-Irish like Williams and most of his peers, said of the Gila country in the 1830s, "This was the freest country on earth at that time. No civilization, laws or books."

One by one, the great concentrations of beaver began to disappear in the early nineteenth century. By 1831 the Atlantic coast beaver had been nearly exterminated, with the few survivors, in the words of the aptly named nineteenth-century theologian John God-man, "like the degraded descendants of aboriginals of our soil, occasionally exhibited as melancholy mementoes of tribes long previously whelmed in the fathomless gulf of avarice." Scarcely three years later the beaver population of the Great Plains was similarly extirpated, and by 1840 the beavers of the interior West's waterways were nearly gone as well. At the time of the European arrival in North America there were some four hundred million beaver on the continent; by 1850 the number stood at a mere nine million. That relative handful remained only because the clipper ship trade to China had newly brought commercial quantities of silk to Europe and the Atlantic seaboard of America, and ladies and gentlemen of fashion now favored this Asian exotic. The trappers drifted into other occupations, becoming mercenaries, wagon-trade guides, and Indian fighters, or they moved on to other animals, notably muskrats and martens. When these, too, had been nearly extinguished, the few remaining trappers shifted to the oceans, organizing the fur-seal companies of the mid-nineteenth century. Frederick Ruxton, an English traveler and secret agent of the time, rightly observed of their combined activities in the West, "Not a hole or corner but has been ransacked by these hardy men."

With the demise of the beaver came a major alteration of the Western landscape. The beaver (*Castor canadensis*) is one of the few animals with the capacity to reshape its environment significantly; because of its engineering talents and sociability, the Apaches believed the beaver to be the wisest of all creatures. Weighing an average of forty-five pounds, the beaver requires prodigious quantities of food for subsistence, favoring the bark and soft flesh of the aspen tree, of which it eats some fifteen hundred pounds yearly, about two hundred trees. Other trees fall before the beaver to form dams, behind which it constructs its famous lodges. Thousands of these impoundments once dotted the Gila, forming reservoirs that helped control seasonal flooding and provided wetlands for migrating birds. When dammed reservoirs were abandoned and, with the eventual breakup of the dams, when the pools dried up, great meadows of tall grass were left in their stead. Ringed by aspen groves and stands of hardwood trees, these natural leas sustained large populations of deer and elk. The remnants of felled trees, for their part, provided shelter for nesting birds and smaller animals. The wholesale destruction of the beaver disrupted these ecological relationships, and for the first time erosion became a major problem as the river flooded unchecked, while animal populations fluctuated wildly as their habitats began to disappear.

The demise of the beaver coincided with the arrival of thousands of Anglos to the Gila basin. Most were westward bound, thanks to the discovery of gold at John Augustus Sutter's California sawmill on January 24, 1848. Only twelve days later the governments of the United States and Mexico signed the Treaty of Guadalupe Hidalgo, formally ending the trumped-up war that Abraham Lincoln called "the most shameful in our history" and ceding what is now the Southwest and California to the victorious Americans. For the next four years the Gila River formed part of the boundary between the two nations. (The Gadsden Purchase of 1852, made in part to mollify Southern congressmen who were agitating to build an intercontinental railroad along the 32nd parallel, established the present border south of the Gila.)

Sutter's discovery prompted hundreds of thousands of Easterners and immigrants to make their way to California and try their fortunes. Rather than undertake the long journey around Cape Horn, many would-be miners sailed from New Orleans to Matamoros, Mexico, at the mouth of the Río Grande, and then proceeded overland to Sonora, swung north along the Santa Cruz River valley, and followed the Gila from the Pima Villages westward to the Colorado. The ancient river route, a Houston newspaper proclaimed, was "so well furnished with good pasturage and water that mules or horses could travel the whole distance without interruption, and the journey could be made in about two months with pack mules and in about three months with wagons."

The Gila route had been surveyed and mapped during the Mexican-American War, when General Philip St. George Cooke's Mormon Battalion traversed northern Sonora in flanking actions against the Mexican garrisons stationed there. Recruited from the Mormon communities of Illinois, the battalion was led across the desert by former mountain men Antoine Leroux, E. Pauline Weaver, and Jean-Baptiste Charbonneau, the métis son of Sacajawea, who had guided the Lewis and Clark expedition across the Northwest. Militarily the battalion's actions were undistinguished, but it does deserve a place in the history books for the single engagement it fought, which has come to be known as the Battle of the Bulls. The conflict took place along the San Pedro River on December 15, 1847.

The antagonists were the men of the Mormon Battalion and a large herd of feral cattle, the descendants of animals the Spaniards had abandoned on their retreat from the Gila in the face of Apache incursions half a century before. The bulls charged; the men fired; and, as a celebratory poem written by Private Levi Hancock recalled,

> *When the fearful fight was o'er*
> *And the sound of muskets heard no more,*
> *At least a score of bulls were found,*
> *And two mules dead upon the ground.*

The wild herd scattered, and the victorious Mormon Battalion— including a young lieutenant who had been gored in the encounter, a sergeant who had been trampled, and a soldier who had shot himself in the thumb—continued westward. Along the way they camped near the Pima Villages, which reminded Cooke "of a crowded New Orleans market," and traded with the Pimas and Maricopas for fresh produce and grains. Cooke was so impressed by the Indians' hospitality that he wrote to Brigham Young to propose that their villages become the final destination of the coming Mormon migration from Illinois. (Fortunately for the Akimel O'odham, Young chose Utah instead.) When the men had rested for a few days the battalion continued on to California, floating a portion of their stores on a Gila-borne raft that caught on sandbars every few miles and eventually had to be abandoned in midstream.

American victory brought the United States a vast new territory, comprising the present states of Arizona, New Mexico, and California, along with portions of Texas, Colorado, Utah, Kansas, Nevada, and Oregon; as President James K. Polk observed on the signing of the Treaty of Guadalupe Hidalgo, the United States was now larger than Europe. Until later military reconnaissances established the potential value of the territory's mineral resources and timber, many in government thought the land to be a howling, impoverished wilderness. The jurist Daniel Webster argued before Congress, "What do we want with this vast worthless area—this region of savages and wild beasts, of shifting sands and whirlwinds of dust, of cactus and prairie dogs? To what use could we ever hope to put those great deserts and endless mountain ranges?" William Tecumseh Sherman, then an army captain, returned from an early survey of the Southwest and responded yet more directly to President Zachary Taylor's questions. Taylor asked Sherman, "Will our new possessions pay for the blood and treasure spent in the war?" Sherman replied, "General, I feel we'll have to go to war again." Taylor asked Sherman why. "To make 'em take the damn country back," he said. Those closer to the field, however, believed that the United States had not gained enough territory from its lopsided victory over Mexico, especially a much-desired seaport on the

The Gila River at its confluence with the Colorado above Yuma, Arizona. A surveyor's error kept the delta of the Colorado out of American hands. (Engraving from John R. Barlett's Personal Narrative, 1854)

northern end of the Gulf of California; because of a surveyor's error, the present international boundary jogs to the northwest where, had it gone straight, it would have cut across the gulf. A quarter-century later the *Yuma Sentinel* editorialized that Washington should have annexed the delta of the Colorado River:

> *The mouth of the Colorado River is fast becoming an unknown country, since the steamboats have stopped running below Yuma. But for its belonging to Mexico, whose government affords no security to life, no encouragement to industry and no protection to property, that country would have long ago been filled up with settlers. The valley is wide, and composed entirely of rich alluvial soil. The climate is superb; the heat of summer is tempered by*

breezes from the gulf; the dry winds of the desert, lying on both sides of the valley, dissipate and oxydize all miasma arising from decay of the rank vegetation. A large part of it is subject to overflow. Extreme tides rise to a height of thirty-five feet; the fresh water of the Colorado is backed up and floods the country for miles. For rice culture no better land can be found. Hemp grows wild in enormous fields subject to occasional overflow. On the higher and drier parts of the valley grow cotton, sugar-cane and tropical fruits, as well as cereals. For the sportsman this country is a paradise. The lagoons formed by the flooding water are filled with fowl. Fish abound in endless variety, from the delicious mullet to the monster jew-fish; hook, net and harpoon can here find unceasing employment. Immense beds supply excellent clams. At the lower part fresh water is comparatively scarce, though the Indians find it readily by digging out seepages along the bank of the sloughs. Hot and mineral springs are found quite near the coast. A feature of the Colorado, near its mouth, is the "bore." This name is given to a high wave, which daily comes rushing in like a wall of water. It is an effect of the tides, and has its parallel in few other rivers of the world. To small boats, or even to steamboats, it brings peril, unless they be skillfully handled. Green turtle abound in the gulf, and occasionally some of these immense chelonians are captured near the mouth of the river. From its isolation this valley has many plants and forms of life peculiar to itself. But just now that book is sealed.

Despite the efforts of freebooters like William Walker, who led a ragtag army of American adventurers into Mexico in 1853 in an unsuccessful attempt to seize the northern states of Baja California and Sonora for the United States, the Colorado Delta would rest in the hands of Mexico.

The Gila Trail was heavily traveled for a decade. In 1849 alone some 75,000 Anglos used it to make their way to California, and today you can follow the ruts made by their wheels in the hard soil of the western Arizona desert. (In 1849, too, the first Anglo child born in Arizona came into the world, his delivery room yet another stranded raft on the river; his given name was Gila.) Apart from its "good pasturage and water," the route was fairly level, making wagon travel relatively easy. However, it passed through infernally hot territory, and to ease their teams' burdens the forty-niners abandoned warehouses full of goods along the riverbank. John Woodhouse Audubon, who followed it in 1850, observed that the Gila Trail was "garnished almost every league with dead cattle, horses, or oxen; and wagons, log chains, and many valuable things are left at almost every camping ground by the travellers." Other forty-niners remarked on older detritus, left behind by the Hohokam five centuries earlier. One, Benjamin Butler Harris, reports, "I discovered several earthen jars half-buried in the earth, which I determined on returning to secure. . . . They were the only ones of myriad fragments of broken pottery noticed by us in this Gila country." Harris also reported the Gila to be waist-deep at the Pima Villages, "full of long, slender trout. . . . Millions of blue quail inhabited near the water."

Although they could scarcely afford to do so, the Akimel O'odham became famous among the forty-niners for their generosity; they provided grain and vegetables to nearly everyone who asked, and after 1849 they increased their fields substantially in order to grow still more surplus food for Anglo travelers. On occasion their generosity was ill repaid. In 1849 John Glanton's notorious gang entered the Pimería in search of the Seven Cities of Cíbola, guided by one Judge Holden, who swore by their existence. They crossed the Gila east of the Pima Villages and made their way into Apache country, from which they were quickly driven. The Apaches had at first been friendly with passing Anglos, whom they regarded as allies in their longstanding enmity against Spain and later Mexico. Their friendship changed to hatred, however, when in 1835 James Johnson, an American trader, called a conference with war chief Juan José at the Santa Rita del Cobre mines near the Gila's headwaters. Johnson was married to a Mexican woman and under the payroll of the governor of Chihuahua, who had charged him with settling the "Apache problem" in any manner he chose.

At the meeting Johnson told Juan José that he had brought a sack of pinole for the women and children, who gathered around it in a tight bunch. One of Johnson's company then fired a six-pound cannon that had been hidden under a mule blanket, its barrel filled with nails, minié balls, glass, and bits of chain. Twenty Apache women died, while dozens more were maimed, and in the ensuing melee four hundred Apaches were killed. Johnson brought down Juan José himself with a pistol shot at close range. (An eyewitness, Benjamin D. Wilson, who had met Juan José while trapping beaver along the Gila, reported the massacre with satisfaction. Wilson later became the first American mayor of Los Angeles, where Johnson would also live to a ripe and apparently remorseless old age.)

In retaliation the Apaches sent off war parties against Mexicans and American trapping parties along the length of the Gila, and the Mexican government responded by commissioning James Kirker, an Irish rebel, to finish Johnson's work. With a band of retired mountain men and Delaware Indians who had been driven from their eastern homelands by Anglo immigration, Kirker roamed Chihuahua and New Mexico gathering scalps. The Apaches matched Kirker death for death, and Glanton and his company were lucky indeed to have left the highlands intact.

Determined to wreak vengeance on any Indian, friendly or not, for the humiliation the Apaches had inflicted, Glanton's gang made its way back to the Pima Villages. One of the gang, a veteran of the Mexican-American War named Samuel Chamberlain, wrote in his memoir *My Confession* that "Glanton, savage and surly, swore that he would assault the place, and give no quarter to man, woman, or child. Holden supported him, but . . . all of the mountain men [who were their guides] not only opposed this cruel massacre but swore it should not take place." Glanton relented, and the gang entered the villages to be met with customary generosity. The Pima rescinded their hospitality, however, when Judge Holden seized a young girl and took "gross liberties with her person"; driven from the villages, the brigands made their way across the desert to Yuma, where they seized control of a Quechan ferry that charged forty-niners a dollar apiece to take them across the flood-swollen Colorado. They had barely enough time to run a few ferryloads of passengers across the river at the new price of four dollars a head when a group of Quechans returned and killed Glanton, sending his headless body afloat to the Gulf of California. The gang was but the advance guard of an army of men whose record, as Mary Austin later put it, "was of violence and destruction; men to whom all Indians were 'varmints' and all Spanish-speaking, 'greasers,' therefore plunderable."

Yet Indian attacks on travelers along the Gila Trail were surprisingly rare. One, however, came to be emblematic of the supposed savagery of the indigenous peoples, and it provoked an increased American military presence throughout the Gila basin. On March 19, 1851, a mixed band of Yavapais and Apaches, perhaps two dozen in all, encountered a well-to-do emigrant family, the Oatmans of Illinois, who had gone ahead of their fifty or so wagon-train companions in their eagerness to reach California. The Indians instantly killed the two adult Oatmans and four of their children. They threw another, a six-

teen-year-old son named Lorenzo, into the Gila from atop a nearby
bluff, and made off with the surviving daughters, fourteen-year-old
Olive Ann and seven-year-old Mary Ann. Lorenzo survived his wounds
and staggered across the desert to the Pima Villages, where he reported
the incident to a party of American soldiers. Because the Oatman Massacre, as it came to be known, took place on the south bank of the
Gila, still in the possession of Mexico, the Americans declared that
they could do nothing.

The Apaches sold the two girls to a Mojave band on the lower
Colorado River, and Olive Ann lived among them for the next five
years, while Mary Ann died of disease at some point during her captivity. For her part Olive Ann was treated as one of the Mojaves, but
when famine hit the Mojave country in 1856 she was ransomed to an
American named Henry Grinnell, who took her to Fort Yuma. There
she became the subject of sensationalist news stories that dwelled on
the ceremonial tattoos with which the Mojaves had adorned her as a
mark of esteem, and soon thereafter the Reverend Royal B. Stratton
published his even more lurid *Captivity of the Oatman Girls*, full of
tales of depraved redskins and unthinkable tortures gleaned from the
vast library of Indian captivity stories published the century before.
Stratton's book raised a public outcry against the supposedly predatory
savages who roamed the Gila country, and before long American cav-
alry patrols rode the river route. For her part, Olive Ann shunned the
publicity as best she could, never taking the opportunity to correct the
fictitious accounts of her five years of captivity. She later married and
lived the remainder of her long life in Sherman, Texas, far from the
Gila country. She kept to herself, but an old friend recalls her wistfully
saying, in her old age, that "she would like to go and see some of her
old friends, even if they were Indians."

Not all travelers along the Gila Trail ended up tattooed or in California. A few enterprising souls, having read Spanish accounts of the

*Olive Ann Oatman, opposite, in the 1860s, her Mohave tattoos
plainly visible.* (Photograph courtesy of the Arizona Historical Society)

Espejo expedition of 1582, during which silver was discovered in
north-central Arizona along the Hassayampa tributary, set claims on
likely sites along the lower Gila. Others reopened the abandoned Santa
Rita del Cobre mine. Still in operation today, by 1807 it produced
20,000 mule loads of copper annually, shipped to the Royal Mint in
Mexico City. The deep forests of the headwaters country paid dearly
for its success, felled to make beams for mineshafts and fuel for ore-
reduction furnaces. To this day the federally protected Gila Wilderness
is dotted with abandoned mines and tailing piles, and is scarred by
clearcutting from the last century.

The boosters succeeded, perhaps beyond their greediest dreams.
In 1851 Francis Aubry of Tucson proclaimed that he had witnessed
Indians along the Hassayampa River firing bullets made of pure gold,
and miners rushed to the Gila to stake out claims. Then, in 1857,
Jacob Snively, Sam Houston's personal secretary during the Texas
Rebellion, discovered gold at a place he called Gila City, a mile and
a half west of the present town of Dome, near Yuma. Newspaper re-
porter J. Ross Browne witnessed the birth and death of the subse-
quent miniature gold rush, described in his *Adventures in the Apache
Country:*

> *Enterprising men hurried to the spot with barrels of whiskey and
> billiards tables; Jews came with ready-made clothing and fancy
> wares; traders crowded in with wagons of pork and beans; and
> gamblers came with cards and Monte tables. There was every-
> thing in Gila City within a few months but a church and a
> jail, which were accounted barbarisms by the mass of the popu-
> lation.*

Seven years later, Browne reported, nothing was left but "three chimneys and a coyote," and Gila City became the first of many ghost towns in Arizona.

Mines sprouted all over the Gila basin in the 1850s, and while some produced commercial quantities of precious metals and minerals, most failed. A few notable successes kept miners streaming into the territory: the La Fortuna mine at the south end of the Gila Mountains, near Yuma, produced three million dollars worth of gold in just three years; the King of Arizona mine to the north yielded four million in a decade; and a network of mines in the San Pedro drainage yielded 8 billion pounds of copper, 355 million pounds of zinc, and 2.8 million ounces of gold over ninety years. Many silver mines were richer still: so-called supergene enrichments or "surface bonanzas," by which rainwater concentrated silver chloride near the ground, abounded in the territory.

The mines brought a huge increase in the population in the Gila basin, especially in the Western desert, despite descriptions of the environment that sent most would-be prospectors onward to the milder climes of California. Richard Hinton's *Hand-Book to Arizona*, which boosted settlement in the territory, was especially discouraging in its uncommon moments of candor:

> *From the middle of June to the 1st of October panting humanity finds no relief from the heat. As soon as the sun appears above the horizon its heat is felt, and this continues to increase until a maximum is reached about three o'clock in the afternoon, after which the temperature falls slowly, and oftentimes very slowly, until sunrise. During the hottest part of the day exertion of any kind is impossible; even while lying perfectly quiet the perspiration oozes from the skin and runs from the body in numerous streams. Everything feels hot to the touch, and metallic*

objects cannot be handled without producing blisters upon the skin. The white sand reflects the heat and blinds the traveller by its glare. Rain scarcely ever falls during the summer months, and not more than three or four inches of rain the year round. The atmosphere is so dry and evaporation so rapid that the water in our canteens, if the cover was kept moist, kept a temperature of 30 deg. below that of the air. Great quantities of water are drunk during these hot days, and no uncomfortable fullness is experienced. One gallon per man, and sometimes two, was the daily consumption.

Notwithstanding the excessive heat, no sunstrokes occurred, although we were at one time exposed in a narrow cañon to a temperature of 120 deg. All of the party preserved good health during the summer. There is no danger of catching cold in this climate, even if wet to the skin three or four times during the day or night. No dew or moisture is deposited during the night, hence no covering is required. The hot wind which blows frequently from the south is the most disagreeable feature of the climate. No matter where you go, it is sure to find you out and give you the full benefit of a gust that feels as if it issued from a blast-furnace, and parches the skin and tongue in an instant. Then there is no recourse but to take copious draughts from the canteens to keep up the supply of moisture in the body. If water cannot be obtained, the delirium of thirst soon overpowers the unfortunate traveller, and he dies a horrible death.

Still, the lure of riches kept the stream of miners coming. By 1870 there were 13,000 miners and 6,500 mining operations in the Gila basin. The miners faced their share of disappointments: gold and silver lessened in importance as early supplies played out, and most mines extracted less glamorous materials: the Castle Dome mine yielded

*Miners examining a pan for gold along the Hassayampa River, ca.
1870.* (Photograph courtesy of the Southwest Studies Program, Maricopa
Community College)

eighteen million pounds of lead; other mines yielded cinnabar, zinc,
iron, manganese, and molybdenum; and still others produced great
quantities of the water-soluble minerals associated with deserts around
the world: salt, gypsum, borax, and a wide range of nitrates and phos-
phates. In the 1870s copper became an important ore largely through
the advance of the telegraph, which required copper wires, and the
huge mines at Clifton and Morenci—twin towns near the confluence

of the upper Gila and San Francisco rivers—were born. For the first decade there were no smelters in the Gila basin, and the ore had to be shipped by rail to New York and thence to Wales to be smelted and then shipped back to America.

In a few years these and other mines had stripped away whole mountains, diverted rivers for hydraulic mining, and chewed up great forests. Owing to the instability of the world's metal markets, miners were just as easily used up, kept on in good years and let go in bad ones. Those who tried to organize to prevent such caprice were gunned down for their troubles in places like Tombstone and Silver City; others were replaced by immigrants from Chihuahua, *los mineros*, who mine owners regarded as "cheap, docile" labor. Even these would revolt, as in 1903 in Clifton. The months-long strike was broken only by a flood of the San Francisco River that destroyed the town. History would repeat itself in 1983, when yet another Clifton strike was smashed by yet another devastating flood.

Despite labor troubles, the mines continued to call for workers, recruiting from as far afield as Cornwall and the Balkan States. Handbills and prospectuses flew out of the New York headquarters of mining concerns like Phelps-Dodge, extolling the abundance of the Southwest and seeking investment capital as well as docile workers:

> *Mills and smelting works are still urgently needed in every mining district; and with competent managers are certain to pay a liberal percentage on the capital invested. . . . If capitalists will invest money in enterprises such as these, bringing solid and certain returns, it would be not only far more desirable for the community, but better for themselves than when put into stocks, land-grabs, and other forms of respectable gambling. Gold, silver, copper, lead, iron, coal, a bracing climate, a fertile soil,*

> *irrigating facilities over a large area only needing develop-*
> *ment—these constitute a combination of natural resources only*
> *needing roads, capital, and labor to make Arizona the richest*
> *State in the Union.*

Today mining continues to take its toll on the Gila, for the General Mining Law of 1872 has never been revised. Antiquated in its own time, this destructive act declared that "mineral deposits are free and open to exploration and purchase," and miners then and now are able to purchase land where minerals were found at homestead prices, almost never exceeding $5.00 an acre; a would-be miner needs only to go to the county courthouse and file claim for twenty acres, immediately redeemable. Nearly two million claims have been filed on the public lands of the West.

The evidence of this economically marginal work is everywhere, in the form of countless abandoned mines, tailings piles, arsenic- and cyanide-poisoned aquifers, and sulfurous skies. Mining claims are even recognized in national parks—uranium exploration still takes place in Grand Canyon—and most commercial mining takes place on public lands that are supposedly under the protection of the Bureau of Land Management. Attempts to change the situation have been summarily defeated: in 1992, for example, a group of congressmen introduced legislation to require that mines pay royalties of 5 to 12.5 percent for the use of public lands. Saying that such fees "could seriously threaten the economic viability of mining projects," the metals industry successfully lobbied to defeat the bill.

Today mine owners are excused from laws governing other toxic industries. In the town of Globe, along the middle Gila, worker housing was built atop asbestos tailings, and when these workers began to develop unusual cancers at unusually high rates, the mines simply dismissed them. Downstream, the giant ASARCO smelter at Hayden, which produces 175,000 tons annually of extremely high-grade copper, also yields one of the nation's highest concentrations of airborne arsenic. The smelter's state air-pollution permit expired in March 1985, and the Arizona government has yet to bother to press for its renewal. In the meanwhile, thanks to George Bush's weakening of the Clean Air Act of 1990, ASARCO has until the year 2000 to reduce emissions—and then only nominally.

The Gila River had borne few scars before. An onslaught of economic expansion a century and a half ago began to change its face forever. And the work of the trappers and miners was only a start.

The history of man is a series of conspiracies
to win from Nature some advantage
without paying for it.
—RALPH WALDO EMERSON

6

THE TIGHTENING
NOOSE

The historic Akimel O'odham had a rich proverbial literature, but it seems not to have included the equivalent of the Anglo observation that no good deed goes unpunished. For years they had practiced what Bernard De Voto called "the communism of the desert," handing out cornmeal cakes and water to passing travelers at the expense of their own stomachs; for their generosity their villages, as Captain William Emory noted, were full of "Pimos, Maricopas, Mexicans, French, Dutch, English, and Americans" who had come to exchange cloth and beads for Akimel O'odham tobacco and foodstuffs, and, not coincidentally, to fill their bellies. As farmers who unknowingly inherited techniques and seed stock from the Hohokam, the river people had long been able to grow a full crop on a single irrigation (which is now impossible, thanks to the weaker genetic resources of hybridized sweet corn and wheat stocks), and they usually had an abundance of food. Still, by the 1860s, their open-handedness threatened to overwhelm the Akimel O'odham with uninvited guests, the numbers of which seemed endless.

Unlike most Native American groups, they enjoyed a fine reputation among the Anglos. One glowing notice came from a member of the Mormon Batallion, who wrote of the Pima, "To us it was a rare sight to be thrown in the midst of a large nation of what are termed wild Indians surpassing many of the Christian nations in agriculture, little behind them in the useful arts and immeasurably before them in honesty and virtue." His description did not go unnoticed among the hierarchy of the infant Church of Jesus Christ of Latter-Day Saints (LDS), whose leaders Philip St. George Cooke had already alerted to the rich possibilities of Mormon settlement along the Gila. Having arrived in their Kingdom of Deseret, now the state of Utah, only in 1847, the Mormons were slow to colonize neighboring territories; they had enough to do fighting plagues of locusts and otherwise subduing their new homeland. When in 1862 the U.S. government effectively declared war on the sect by passing laws against the Mormon practice of bigamy, however, church leader Brigham Young, a brilliant strategist by all accounts, ordered a number of his followers to lay out towns stringing southward and northward from Salt Lake City, each a day's ride from the next. This network would assure the possibility of a well-provisioned flight to either Canada or Mexico should the need arise.

These towns were established in time, and their founders came well prepared for almost any contingency. By the late 1860s the Mormons had founded several towns along the fertile bottomlands of the middle Gila, notably Safford and Florence, Arizona—at the time the two towns constituted the largest settlement of Mormons outside Utah—and had colonized nearly the whole of the Little Colorado River to the near north. From Brigham Young himself they carried the order to "make the desert blossom."

It was no mere slogan. Years before the Mormons left Illinois for Utah, their leaders had dispatched emissaries to study drylands agriculture and irrigation practices; Brigham Young had planned the great migration in every detail by 1845, two years before the supposedly divinely ordained flight to the intermontane promised land. One of his chief emissaries was Orson Hyde, who had toured Mediterranean Europe and the Near East in 1840 to report on irrigation methods. The notes he made on the great Moorish waterworks and aqueducts that dotted Spain, as well as the gravity-canal systems of Palestine and Egypt, underlay the church's subsequent water policies. The Mormon Batallion's time in New Mexico reinforced Hyde's observations, for Moorish *acequia* irrigation still flourished there, virtually unchanged in local practice. Wrote one wide-eyed member of the force, the New Mexicans' "mode of living & farming is Singular enough to me but they Seem to get along & Seem to be happy enough. . . . On account of the dry Seasons in this country they have to irrigate all this farming land all their vineyards & orchards which is done by leading the water from the River through ditches through all their grain & every thing else that is raised."

Young's commandment came from a strident belief, derived from the Old Testament, that humans had an obligation to subdue the earth to their advantage. John Widtsoe, an LDS leader, elaborated, "The destiny of man is to possess the whole earth; the destiny of the earth is to be subject to man. There can be no full conquest of the earth, and no real satisfaction to humanity, if large portions of the earth remain beyond his highest control." (To this day, honoring Widtsoe's dictum, the Mormon church opposes the call to create new wilderness areas in the West.) Everywhere they went the Mormons altered the landscape. If you drive through the badlands of Navajo country to the north of the Gila basin and notice windbreaks of slender Lombardy poplars planted in the unlikeliest places—atop seemingly unscalable mesas, amid great ergs of red sand—you will have witnessed the ruins of the first Mormon settlements.

The LDS colonists set about putting as much land as they could into service, for they had a new nation to feed. To do so they worked from a strict system of communal labor, sharing the agricultural toil and rewards alike in an idyll that would soon collapse in most particulars. They shared the resources around them as well. Borrowing from Moorish Spain, as had the neighboring New Mexicans, the Mormons established the rotating office of Water Master, who had near-dictatorial powers with respect to the desert's most valuable treasure. As Virginia Sorensen recalls in *Where Nothing Is Long Ago*, her beautifully written memoir of a Mormon desert girlhood,

> *Each household in town had its own dam—often nothing more than a couple of boards with a short handle nailed to them— and its own water turn when the dam was put to use. Set across the streams in the streetside ditches, and packed in with wet turf, these dams were sufficient to turn the water onto lawns and gardens, and nothing short of a calamity could prevent a householder from putting in his dam at the proper time. Every spring, the Water Master—an official of great importance in a Utah town—provided each family with a list of Water Turns, carefully worked out. We always kept our list tacked inside the door of the kitchen cupboard.*

These "water turns" were so strictly observed, Sorensen continues, that when one of the Mormon brethren cut into line and was subsequently killed for his transgression, the murder was excused as justifiable homicide.

But the Mormons had few qualms about taking water from its original "owners," the river people. Native Americans were, in Mormon doctrine, the "Lamanite" lost tribespeople of Israel, supposedly the beneficiaries of Jesus Christ's resurrection in the Americas. In daily fact, however, the Mormons despised them. "The Indians were uncivilized," remarked Golden Buchanan, who, ironically, headed the Mormon church's Indian Placement Office. "They didn't know how to take care of themselves. The way they lived was atrocious. You couldn't be friends with an Indian and keep your self-respect." For all the hostility, though, Brigham Young discouraged his followers from taking up arms against the unfortunate Lamanites, remarking, "It is cheaper to feed the Indians than to fight them." In saying so he ignored, of course, the Indians' well-attested ability to feed themselves, and he set another course for a legacy of dependence.

Within a dozen years of their arrival in the Gila Valley, the Mormons of Safford, on the middle Gila, and Florence, about a hundred river miles downstream, had dammed the river to flood their fields. Their engineering projects proved so successful that by 1873 the Akimel O'odham—who seven years earlier had sold the U.S. Army five million pounds of surplus wheat from their fields at the Pima Villages—could not irrigate their fields sufficiently to feed themselves, let alone the travelers who continued to stream by their homes. Suspecting that sorcery lay behind this catastrophe and the increase of virulent diseases that coincidentally accompanied it, the Akimel O'odham killed three shamans in the village of Sacaton. Still the waters were not forthcoming, and so a delegation of Akimel O'odham traveled east to Washington, where, after they waited for some weeks, President Ulysses S. Grant finally received them. Their nominal leader, Antonio Azul, put their case bluntly:

> *For hundreds of years my people have lived along the banks of the Gila River. We have always been honest and peaceful and have supported ourselves and never asked for any help from the*

Great White Father in Washington. Until the past few years we have always had plenty of water to irrigate our farms and never knew what want was. We always had grain stored up for a full year's supply. We were happy and contented. Since the white man came and built the big canals and ditches, we have no water for crops. The government refuses to give us food and we do not ask for it. We can only ask for water, for we prefer to earn our own living if we can.

In response, Grant suggested that the Pimas migrate to Oklahoma, which was then still called the Indian Territory, and negotiate a new homeland with the dominant Cherokee and Creek residents there. When Antonio Azul made it plain that the Akimel O'odham would not leave their ancestral homeland—pointedly reminding Grant of the tribe's aid to the Union cause—the president grudgingly agreed to supply the Pima with the grain they needed. In coming to his decision Grant may well have wondered whether the Pima, a pacific nation, had finally found cause to take up arms against the United States. After two decades of fighting the Apaches had only recently been quieted, and he abhorred the prospect of fighting a new enemy.

It had taken fully a quarter of the standing army of the United States to break Diné power. Ever since James Johnson's betrayal of Juan José, most Apaches had in the main regarded Anglos as their enemies, just as they did Mexicans, and for half a century the Gila corridor became a battleground. The Apaches fought a steady guerrilla campaign, focusing on lone travelers and isolated ranches and farms, while the Americans relied on treachery as much as on superior arms. Indeed, the history of the Apache wars offers a litany of betrayals. One of the most notable occurred in January 1863, when the former mountain man Joseph Reddeford Walker lured Mangas Coloradas (Red

Sleeves) to Pinos Altos, New Mexico, for a supposed peace parley. Congress had three years earlier authorized the creation of an Apache reservation at the headwaters of the Gila, and Walker assured Mangas that he merely wished to work out the details of relocating his people there. Instead, American soldiers murdered Mangas Coloradas and several of his followers; an eyewitness reported that "a little soldier, calling himself John T. Wright, scalped Mangas with an Arkansas toothpick [that is, a Bowie knife]." Wright then removed Mangas Coloradas's head, boiled the skull to remove the skin, and sent his trophy to the East. (It has never been recovered, and some Apaches believe that Mangas's headless ghost yet awaits trespassers in their domain.) Had the parley been genuine, the statesmanlike Mangas Coloradas may well have concluded a peace, but his murder instead created a generation of Apache military leaders whose gifts for the art of war were unparalleled on this continent.

Recognizing the harm that his troops had done, President Abraham Lincoln recalled the region's commanding general, James Carleton, who had been pestering him for reinforcements. "If I had only one more good regiment of California infantry," Carleton had written, "composed, as that infantry is, of practical miners, I would place it in the Gila country. While it would exterminate the Indians, who are a scourge to New Mexico, it would protect people who might wish to go there to open up the country, and would virtually be a military colony when the [Civil] war ended, whose interests would lead the officers and soldiers to remain in the new El Dorado."

The notion of granting the Apaches a single reservation had been bandied about for years. As early as 1853 John Walker, an Indian agent, had convinced a war leader named Chino Peña to relocate his band from the mineral-rich Pinal Mountains above Globe, Arizona, to the Mogollon Rim near the present town of Show Low; as Walker wrote to his overseer in Washington, "because no settlements yet encroach on their territory, all they will need for a few years will be a liberal distribution of presents yearly and some hoes and spades to enable them to cultivate the soil more extensively." Peña's band at least had something of a choice. The remaining Apaches in the vicinity of Globe and Clifton, in the heart of the so-called Copper Basin alongside the Gila, were simply ordered to relinquish their lands to the mining companies. The agent in charge gathered the chiefs, gave each a hundred Mexican pesos, and demanded that they sign a contract giving up the southernmost portions of their territory—later ceded to the Apaches as the San Carlos Reservation—"or troops would be sent to kill them." These bands settled in the area around Forestdale, near the headwaters of the White River, for a few years but were soon driven out by encroaching Mormon farmers.

The next Apache war leader to find his trust betrayed was Cochise, who was married to Mangas Coloradas's youngest daughter. Wrongly accused in 1861 of rustling Anglo cattle and kidnapping a young *Apache manso,* or "tame Apache," Cochise and his band of Chiricahua Apaches were held hostage by U.S. soldiers against the return of the boy. He and most of his followers managed to escape, taking hostages as they fled southward, but the pursuing soldiers took their vengeance by killing every Apache they encountered, perhaps a dozen in all. In retaliation, Cochise set about raiding farms throughout the upper Gila drainage, later turning his attention to stagecoaches along the Butterfield line. Cochise kept up his campaign until 1872, when General Oliver O. Howard, whom President Grant had commissioned to end the war, promised him that the government would establish a reservation in the band's original domain, the Chiricahua Mountains. (General Gordon Granger had six years earlier promised Cochise the same thing, and his reneging on that promise led to another six years of warfare.) Cochise died of cancer not long afterward, and the remaining Chiricahuas, rather than receive the reservation they had been promised, were divided among the San Carlos Apache Reservation, along the middle Gila, and the Mescalero Apache Reservation in southern New Mexico. Cochise may have divined the betrayal, and he surely foresaw that the power of the Diné would be displaced:

> *When I was young I walked all over this country, east and west, and saw no other people than the Apaches. After many summers I walked again and found another race of people had come to take it. . . . The Apaches were once a great nation, but now they are few, and because of this they want to die. . . . Tell me, if the Virgin Mary has walked throughout all the land, why has she never entered the wigwam of the Apache? Why have we never seen or heard her?*

Along the middle Gila, near its confluence with the San Pedro, a band of Aravaipa Apaches had long enjoyed the freedom of the country. In the summer they made the home in the tall, ponderosa-pine–clad mountains; in the winter they camped along river bottoms and narrow canyons, where both game and protection abounded. The Aravaipa had never, so far as is known, committed acts of war against the Anglo farmers who were then streaming into their territory—they reserved their enmity for Mexicans and O'odham—but the federal government determined that they should be confined as prisoners of war, under their own recognizance, on a single encampment near Aravaipa Creek on the middle San Pedro. The band, led by an elder named Eskiminzin, submitted peacefully, and from time to time soldiers from nearby Camp Grant rode out to take a head count and ascertain that their charges were up to no mischief.

This was not enough for the leading citizens of Tucson, the largest town in the region, who were howling for Apache blood regardless of its provenance. When the regional military commandant made it clear that the Aravaipa would remain on their informal reservation under federal protection, two of the city's civic leaders, William Oury and Jesús María Elías, gathered a force of ninety-two Tohono O'odham, forty-two Mexicans, and six Anglos. At dawn on April 30, 1871, this company attacked Eskiminzin's band, and eyewitness accounts of what would come to be called the Camp Grant Massacre attest to their savagery: one ten-month-old Aravaipa boy had his leg hacked off; several women were raped and then shot point-blank in the face; elders were chopped to bits or mashed into pulp with heavy war clubs. By the end of the attack 144 Aravaipa lay dead, but Eskiminzin was not among them, he and a few young men having managed to escape to a side canyon. Most of the dead, a journalist on the scene reported, were in fact children, but few of his Anglo readers were sympathetic. A common expression of the time, "nits make lice," provided all the rationale needed to justify killing Apache women and children.

Outraged, President Grant demanded that Oury and Elías be brought to justice for their part in the slaughter. A Tucson jury deliberated for precisely nineteen minutes before declaring the two and their hirelings innocent of all charges. Fourteen years later, a triumphant Oury would remind his fellow Tucsonans of his works in a signed newspaper editorial:

> *Behold the happy results immediately following that episode. The farmers of San Pedro returned with their wives and babes to gather their abandoned crops. On the Sonoita, Santa Cruz, and all other settlements of southern Arizona, new life springs up, confidences are restored and industry bounds forward with an impetus that has known no check in the fourteen years since that*

occurrence. In view of all these facts, I call on all Arizonans to answer on their conscience—can you call the killing of the Apaches on the morning of April 30th, 1871, a massacre?

Putatively for their protection, the War Department directed that all Apaches be confined to a consolidated reservation. The chosen site, San Carlos, lay along the Gila River some forty miles west of the Mormon town of Safford. For the next four years the army's unenviable task was to ferret out Apaches from their highland camps and march them to the reservation, which the soldiers had dubbed "Hell's Forty Acres." Those Apaches who did not comply were gunned down, the fate of some seventy Yavapai Apache women and children at the so-called Skeleton Cave Massacre of December 1872; many of those who did comply perished en route to starvation or exposure. John Gregory Bourke, an army captain, bitterly recalled the relocations in his memoir *On the Border with Crook*: "It was an outrageous proceeding, one for which I should still blush had I not long since gotten over blushing at anything the United States Government did in Indian matters." A thousand Apaches died in the process, while six thousand or so were finally herded onto the San Carlos Reservation.

One of them conceived a special hatred for the Americans. Called Goyahkla, "The One Who Yawns," he is better known by the name the Mexicans gave him, Geronimo. He was born near the source of the Gila River in about 1823, and he would often return to his natal ground in adulthood, fleeing the pursuing U.S. army, to roll on the ground and thus cloak himself with his ancestral dirt. Trained as a shaman, he had been an unforgiving warrior since his early manhood, after Mexican soldiers who had come to the headwaters murdered his mother, wife, and three children. Until the mid-1860s he had confined

Goyahkla, opposite, "The One Who Yawns," better known by the nom
de guerre *Geronimo.* (Photograph by C. S. Fly, ca. 1885)

his hatred to Mexicans, but the campaign against Cochise focused Geronimo's enmity on the Anglos who were pouring into the Pinos Altos
region on a mad search for gold.

Geronimo and his band went to the San Carlos Reservation peacefully enough. He even consented to their wearing brass dogtags and
presenting themselves for a daily roll call—hateful concessions for a
free people. But eventually Geronimo could not stay put, and he and
his band took to leaving the reservation to hunt at the headwaters of
the Gila, barely a hundred miles away.

U.S. soldiers followed, meaning to arrest Geronimo, but he and
a handful of followers slipped across the border and made their way
to the Sierra Madre of Mexico. From there Geronimo conducted a
brilliant guerrilla campaign that in time would embrace most of Chihuahua and Sonora, as well as southern Arizona and New Mexico.
Still, his numbers dwindled while those of his enemies grew, and when
in 1883 General George Crook came into the mountains to talk peace,
Geronimo was willing to negotiate. He would stop fighting, he said,
if he could return to his homeland. Three years later, after one or two
subsequent outbreaks, Geronimo surrendered to Crook's successor,
Nelson Miles.

He would not see the Gila again. Instead, Geronimo and his followers were shipped off to Fort Marion, Florida, an island compound
where Eskiminzin and the male survivors of the Camp Grant Massacre
were also interned. Within a few years most of the Apaches had died
of tropical diseases, and by 1905 Geronimo could stand it no longer.
He dictated a letter to President Theodore Roosevelt, pleading to be
released:

[The Gila] is my land, my home, my father's land, to which I now ask to be allowed to return. I want to spend my last days there, and be buried among these mountains. If this could be I might die in peace, feeling that my people, placed in their native homes, would increase in numbers, rather than diminish as at present, and that our name would not become extinct.

Roosevelt refused his request, but soon afterward ordered that Geronimo be sent to Fort Sill, Oklahoma, where at least an occasional northeast-tending breeze might carry some hint of New Mexico. For four years Geronimo made for a popular tourist attraction, sitting at the steering wheel of a Cadillac sedan bedecked in a top hat or a Plains Indian headdress. When death came to him on February 17, 1909, at the age of eighty-five, it must have been a relief.

The Apaches were a broken nation. Long used to wandering the river valleys and mountains of the Southwest, they turned to the alien economy of agriculture. They raised hay and barley for the horses of the government that confined them, as well as hundreds of thousands of tons of potatoes, melons, squash, beans, and pumpkins that went to market in nearby Anglo cities and towns. For all their productivity, Apaches continued to die, the victims of diseases like malaria and typhus and especially of hunger; as John Gregory Bourke thoughtfully remarked, "Our government had never been able to starve any of them until it had them placed on a reservation." Many Apaches went to work as government loggers as well, clearing vast portions of the reservation highlands; up until the 1940s Apache sawyers processed some 38 million board feet of native lumber each year.

Apache culture suffered as much as Apache bodies, for the government banned such important rites as the Changing Woman ceremony, fearful that the Apaches might be inspired to rise up against their captors. As late as the 1930s Apache children were cordoned off in barbed-wire compounds for the crime of speaking Diné at government schools, or made to wear a ball and chain for failing to give sufficient respect to the flag or the cross.

The Akimel O'odham fared little better, although they kept their ancestral lands. Year by year Mormon farmers turned more and more of the Gila's waters to their fields upstream; year by year Pima fields, disorderly patches of white dust, failed to yield enough food to sustain their owners. In 1873, an event marked on tribal calendar sticks, a few hundred Akimel O'odham abandoned their lands and moved north to the Salt River valley, where water was still plentiful, lured there by Mormons who wanted a buffer against Apache attacks. The Anglo farmers, of course, enjoyed the profit of these Akimel O'odham labors. At the same time, they were able to annex the abandoned farmlands along the Gila.

By 1880 the government was giving 225,000 pounds of wheat to the inhabitants of the Pima Villages each year. By 1887 the Mormon diversion dams at Florence had turned nearly the entire river away from its course, and only a quarter of the Akimel O'odham's once extensive fields were arable. Entries on Pima calendar sticks began to record, year by year, famine and pestilence. By the turn of the century, during a period of continent-wide Native American religious revival, an Akimel O'odham shaman had delivered an eschatological prophesy from the creator god I'itoi to his people, revealing that their time had passed, that the Anglos would destroy the ancient Pimería:

> *You will not be the ones to kill the staying earth.*
> *I will leave it to them,*
> *And they will do it.*
> *And these will kill the staying earth,*

And even if you don't know anything,
And you will just be feeling fine,
And you will see it
When it happens.

There are very few living Akimel O'odham who saw that gradual destruction of the staying earth. An especially eloquent witness was George Webb, who died in 1965, and who recorded the old ways in his memoir *A Pima Remembers*. Webb farmed a plot of land along the Gila until 1938, when the recently completed Coolidge Dam finally strangled the last of the water out of the Gila; he then opened a grocery store at Gila Crossing—where the river was once three-quarters of a mile wide—and set about writing his life story. His account of a mesquite forest that the Pima called New York Thicket (because the dense trees, they imagined, resembled the skyscraper-studded horizon of the city), three miles wide and eight miles long, provides a heartbreaking précis of the Gila's fate:

In the old days, on hot summer nights, a low mist would spread over the river and the sloughs. Then the sun would come up and the mist would disappear. On those hot nights the cattle often gathered along the river up to their knees in the cool mud.

Soon some Pima boy would come along and dive into the big ditch and swim for awhile. Then he would get out and open the headgate and the water would come splashing into the laterals and flow out along the ditches. By this time all the Pimas were out in the fields with their shovels. They would fan out and lead the water to the alfalfa, along the corn rows, and over to the melons. The red-wing blackbirds would sing in the trees and fly down to look for bugs along the ditches. Their song always *means that there is water close by as they will not sing if there is not water splashing somewhere.*

The green of those Pima fields spread along the river for many miles in the old days when there was plenty of water.

Now the river is an empty bed full of sand.

Now you can stand in that same place and see the wind tearing pieces of bark off the cottonwood trees along the dry ditches.

The dead trees stand there like white bones. The red-wing blackbirds have gone somewhere else. Mesquite and brush and tumbleweeds have begun to turn those Pima fields back into desert.

Now you can look across the valley and see the green alfalfa and cotton spreading for miles on the farms of white people who irrigate their land with hundreds of pumps running night and day. Some of those farms take their water from ditches dug hundreds of years ago by Pimas, or the ancestors of Pimas. Over there across the valley is where the red-wing blackbirds are singing today.

The fields of the white men grew and grew. Unhindered by Apache raiders and encouraged by liberal homestead laws that allowed claims of 160 acres for each farm, large numbers of Anglos set down stakes in the Salt and Gila river valleys. Their way was prepared by John Swilling, "the Father of Phoenix," who had drifted eastward from Gila City in 1858, spied for the Confederacy, and then organized the so-called Gila Rangers in 1864 to fight the Yavapai Apache. Swilling recognized that the Hohokam ditches were irrigation canals, and he restored several miles' worth to sell to newcomer farmers. He made a good sum of money, but addictions to laudanum and alcohol depleted his purse, and in 1878 he unsuccessfully tried to rob a Butter-

*Jack Swilling, opposite, "the Father of Phoenix," as he appeared in
the mid-1880s.* (Photograph courtesy of the Arizona Historical
Foundation)

field stagecoach. Locked up in the Yuma Territorial Prison, Swilling died of typhus, still nursing dreams of creating a canal city to rival Venice.

Many farmers consolidated their holdings in agricultural cooperatives, the forerunners of the industrial farms that dot the region today. None was quite so successful, however, as that founded by one James Addison Reavis, a dapper con man who wandered into the newly founded city of Phoenix in 1884 and proclaimed himself the heir to ten thousand square miles of the Arizona Territory.

As evidence Reavis produced a deed supposedly signed by King Ferdinand VI of Spain, who in 1746, or so Reavis's story went, awarded his Mexican wife's ancestor Miguel de Peralta de Cordoba nearly the whole of Arizona from the banks of the Gila south, including dozens of mines and rich agricultural holdings. After deliberating for a short time, the territorial court decided that Reavis's claim was valid, and the self-styled Baron of Arizona set up shop at an old railroad watering station called Arizola, near the Gila River crossing on Interstate 10 between Tucson and Phoenix. He merrily sold off portions of his estate to hundreds of its earlier owners, earning a fortune in the process. Because he owned the deed to some of Arizona's largest cities at the time—Globe, Florence, and Casa Grande among them—he had no shortage of customers. For twelve years Reavis lived a life of splendor, occasionally deigning to leave his mansion to drive about his fiefdom in an ornate carriage that he had had imported from England. As time passed, his regal arrogance earned him many enemies.

One was Tom Weedin, the editor of the *Florence Citizen*, the region's leading newspaper. Weedin suspected a hoax from the start and wrote thundering editorials denouncing Reavis. But certain prominent Arizonans, glad to have a royal presence in their midst, threatened to withdraw their advertising if Weedin continued his one-man campaign against Reavis, and he moved on to other topics.

In 1893 Weedin's printer went to Phoenix on a weekend holiday and, on a hunch, looked up the Peralta deed. He noticed that the supposedly ancient document was set in a typeface that had only recently been invented, and that another bore the watermark of a Wisconsin paper mill. Weedin reported these details in his paper, and Reavis's game was up. The Baron of Arizona was convicted of forgery in 1895 and was sentenced to six years in the New Mexico Territorial Prison in Santa Fe; the comparatively light term may have reflected the general mood of embarrassment that followed Weedin's discovery. (At about the same time, the courts uncovered a similar fraudulent land grant in California, supposedly giving title to most of the San Francisco Bay Area to one José Yves Limantour.) Paroled after two years, Reavis made his way to California, dying penniless in Los Angeles in 1914. His memory is enshrined only in a few history books and in Samuel Fuller's 1950 feature film *The Baron of Arizona*, where a villainous Vincent Price chews up the scenery in the role of Reavis.

Reavis's fall opened many of the lands of the Gila basin to a renewed wave of Anglos. They mainly settled on the fertile lands between the Salt and Gila rivers, where a chain of Mormon farming hamlets gave way to bustling towns. The western deserts, through which the Gila now only intermittently flowed, proved to be less attractive, but boosters nonetheless promoted settlement there. In his *Hand-book to Arizona*, Richard Hinton wrote of the supposed fertility of the region around Gila City, now dotted with abandoned mines and ghost towns:

James Addison Reavis, the so-called Baron of Arizona. (Photograph courtesy of the Arizona Historical Society)

[Gila City] now consists of a comfortable stage station, a broad expanse of tillable valley land, sometimes overflowed by the river, which is at times "mighty uncertain," and a steep range of volcanic hills coming close to the highways—[the terrain] is for a dozen miles or so hot, heavy and sandy. It is hardly fair to say sandy, as it is really a friable alluvial loam of grayish hue and loose texture. Several ranches are passed, showing that the Gila bottom is cultivable. With irrigation every square mile of the Gila valley is capable of producing prolific crops of grains and semi-tropical fruits, as well as cotton and sugar in great abundance. The river is able to furnish all the water needed, and a good deal more. It would take no very great skill in engineering, and not a very large sum of money either, to construct reservoirs or lakes in which to receive and store the overflow. There are natural basins or dry lakes into which, by simple means, the water could be conveyed. An atmosphere of wonderful richness and brilliance covers the scene like a gorgeous canopy of prismatic colors, and the vision is lost in the immensity of the distances.

Farmers who made their way to the lower Gila seldom found the situation quite so idyllic. Still, they set about churning up the hard desert pan with their plows, and prayed that their labors would yield a promised land.

"Arizona needs only water and climate to make it a Paradise," one local booster proclaimed, to which a local wag responded, "Yes, and that's all hell needs, too." The realities of life in the drylands squared poorly with the claims of the promoters, but few Anglo farmers were willing to alter their practices to conform to the American continent's great absolute: in most places west of the hundredth meridian, water supplies simply do not permit large-scale agriculture.

John Wesley Powell was one of the first Anglo surveyors of the region to recognize this truth. In the summer of 1869, Powell, who six years earlier had lost an arm to wounds suffered at the Battle of Shiloh, led a party of hunters, trappers, and scientists down the Colorado River from the Uinta Valley of Utah to the confluence of the Virgin River west of the Grand Canyon, the first documented river journey through the Grand Canyon. Powell later headed both the U.S. Geological Survey and the Bureau of Ethnology, organizations that well suited his encyclopedic interests, and wrote several studies of the Southwest, including one submitted to the U.S. Congress in 1879, *Lands of the Arid Regions of the United States.* Bernard De Voto, the distinguished Western conservationist and social critic, rightly called it "the most prophetic book in the range of American experience."

Powell noted that the entire system of water law in the West defied the practical realities of the place. At the time of the first Anglo arrivals, water was distributed by common riparian law, derived from the customs of water-rich England by way of the water-rich American East: anyone who settled alongside a river had a right to a share of its water; anyone who lived near but not along the river had secondary rights, but at least was entitled to a share. In the next decade the doctrine of riparian rights was replaced by the doctrine of prior appropriation: whoever got to a river first had rights to it. Naturally, this encouraged settlers to lay claim hurriedly to the Southwest's scant riverlands, thereby depriving their fellows from a supply of water. As the U.S. Revised Statutes of 1877 declared, "When any ditch or acequia shall be taken out for agricultural purposes, the person or persons so taking out such ditch or acequia shall have exclusive right to the water, or so much as may be necessary for such purpose." A settler upstream who diverted water from a river to water his crops, as had the Mormons at Florence and Safford, thus acted within the bounds of the law.

Powell decried this development. Instead of allowing private ownership of the West's scarcest resource, he proposed a division of the arid lands into irrigation districts, with each farmer allowed 80 acres, half the current allotment; no single farmer could reasonably hope to till 160 acres with scant water supplies in any event. These districts, he argued, should conform to topography—one, for example, might lie along the Gila from the Colorado confluence to the rise of the highlands just east of Florence, comprising the low desert—and should be self-governing; that is to say, they should take the place of states. The role of the federal government, he argued, should be confined to providing military protection for settlers and Native Americans alike, and to administer the public lands.

Radical proposal followed radical proposal. Powell argued that private ownership of mountain forests be eliminated, and that no cattle be allowed on public lands. Above all, he suggested that irrigation projects be developed sparingly, only insofar as the natural carrying capacities of rivers would allow.

Powell's arguments met with derision in every congressional committee before which he appeared. The notion of the quarter section of 160 acres as the basis of agrarian democracy had become sacrosanct, artificial as it was; never mind that of 550,000 homestead claims filed, only 200,000 were ever held to full title, the rest of the farmers having failed for one reason or another. His plan was dismissed, and when it was, Powell thundered to a roomful of government officials, "I tell you gentlemen, you are piling up a heritage of conflict and litigation over water rights, for there is not sufficient water to supply the land."

Instead, Congress did almost the opposite of what Powell recommended. The Carey Act of 1894 shed responsibility for the maintenance of the public lands, transferring a million acres of federal holdings to individual western states, with the proviso that they be sold to irrigation companies. Those concerns usually failed for lack of operating capital, and soon the states turned to the government once more to demand aid for irrigation projects. They found a president who was willing to listen in Theodore Roosevelt, who set in motion what Powell feared most, a legacy of conflict over water rights that endures to this day. Roosevelt had plenty of supporters, including John W. Noble, a former interior secretary, who prophesied, "A hundred years hence these United States will be an empire such as the world never before saw, and such as will exist nowhere else upon the globe. . . . Irrigation is the magic wand which is to bring about these great changes."

It would indeed bring about transformations such as Noble could hardly have foreseen, forging a superpower in a ravaged land.

And I brought you into a plentiful country,
to eat the fruit thereof and the goodness thereof;
but when ye entered, ye defiled my land,
and made mine heritage an abomination.
—JEREMIAH 1:6

7

DEATH KNELL

The Gila began to dry up with the arrival of Anglo farmers whose thirsty crops included plants not well suited to the desert: Egyptian cotton, soft wheat, and eventually citrus and nuts. The effect was nearly instantaneous. Within a few years of the Gila's being diverted by Mormon planters the bed of the middle and lower river was dry. Sue Summers, who came to Florence with her attorney husband in 1879, wrote of her first stagecoach journey from Casa Grande to their new home, not long after the first Mormon dams had been built:

> *I had heard so much of the raging Gila River, which I now understood we would have to cross before reaching our destination, that I must confess I had a feeling of fear at the prospect of fording it—imagine my astonishment when we came to a halt*

*within a short distance of Florence, and my husband, with an
amusing smile, announced that the huge valley of sand on which
we were resting was the bed of the Gila River.*

Summers would encounter the river in other moods, however, and she
added, "I have seen it since and know it well deserves the name of
'raging' as its waters inundated the land on its south bank, bringing
the flood to the boundaries of Florence," a normally dusty desert
town.

Six years later the Florentines, having subdued the river for the
benefit of their fields, would experience yet another of the river's wiles.
As soon as the town had built its first bridge over the Gila, the river

*The Florence ferry line in its last years, before an auto bridge
connected the Salt River valley to southern Arizona.* (Photograph
courtesy of the Arizona Historical Foundation)

changed course, cutting a meander a hundred yards shy of the gleaming steel structure and rendering it useless. The flood also destroyed the ferry line that had connected Florence to the towns of the Salt River valley to the north.

Industrialized farming changed the face of the Gila basin. Beginning with the Mormon colonization of the fertile middle river, agriculture had provided a strong lure for Anglo settlement; the pacification of the Apaches removed the last great disincentive. In the late nineteenth century, Phoenix-area developers advertised in national farming magazines that farmers were wanted all along the middle Gila, claiming that the region enjoyed plentiful water, "underground reservoirs of unlimited volume," "lost rivers," and "hidden streams" that could never be exhausted.

The farmers came, founding towns like Coolidge and Casa Grande, swelling the population of Phoenix and its satellite communities. The Homestead Act of 1862 had authorized the grant of 160 acres to anyone willing to farm it for five years, and the Gila soon sported a patchwork of small farms that produced beans, corn, tomatoes, melons (Phoenix's original name was Pumpkinville), and other goods. Farmers wrestled with inappropriate technologies, relying at first on the John Deere plow, the ideal tool to turn up the loamy soils of the Midwest but not the crusty soil of the deserts; later they developed plows that were better suited to their purposes. Still, as John Wesley Powell had warned not long before, in the arid West no farmer could hope to farm 160 acres profitably. Only after the development of the "farmall" machine in the early 1900s and, later, of the center-pivot sprinkler was it feasible for a single farmer to cultivate that much land, but even larger farms, in the days before massive agricultural subsidies, generally netted only $100 a year in profit.

Most of the small farmers would not remain long. The advent of the First World War brought with it a worldwide demand for long-staple cotton, used in clothing, tires, airplane fabrics, and munitions; with the demand came the rise of agricultural corporatism in the Southwest. Developers had already begun to buy out small farms all along the middle Gila by 1910, anticipating the completion of Roosevelt Dam on the Salt tributary, and when the war broke out they had replaced the native Pima small-boll cotton with imported Egyptian long-staple varieties. The Goodyear Tire Company established whole towns of cottonfield workers, among them the 24,000-acre hamlet of Egypt, and imported Russian, Japanese, and Mexican workers to perform the labors the resident Anglo population now refused to undertake. The immigrants were required to repay the cost of bringing them to Arizona—often inflated to $100 when a top worker made only $6 a week—and to shop in company stores, and in effect they formed a class of indentured servants who would be freed only by labor reforms under Roosevelt's New Deal. In their camps, where irrigation ditches served as both sewers and the source of drinking water, outbreaks of typhoid and cholera were common; the middle Gila, once the site of numerous sanitariums for the victims of tuberculosis, now became a breeding ground for disease.

By 1920 cotton grew on 200,000 acres of land along the Salt River. The acreage tripled a decade later, with most of the cotton going to England's textile mills. When the market crashed in 1932 during the worldwide economic depression, many of the Gila's large cotton farms were temporarily abandoned. Once again, it took a war to make them profitable anew.

But at great cost. Egyptian cotton, developed along the water-rich Nile, requires annual irrigation to a depth of five feet of water an acre, and upon harvest it must be washed with saltwater and chemical bleaches to strip it of its leaves and open its white bolls. The diversion of so much water meant the death of the Gila below Gila Bend, where the hotter and drier western desert begins; the intensive irrigation and bleaching meant that fields would swiftly be coated, as in Hohokam times, with an impermeable salt crust that would render the land useless. To that old story is added a modern twist: the groundwater beneath agricultural lands now carries vast amounts of toxic pesticides like methyl parathion that have leached through the soil. The lower Gila from the confluence of the Agua Caliente River to Dateland has been placed on the Environmental Protection Agency Superfund cleanup roster because of massive DDT contamination—and DDT has not legally been in use in the United States since 1969.

Even today, cotton is Arizona's greatest crop in terms of both acreage and value. But to add to the Gila's woes, industrial agriculture brought to the Southwest other thirsty nonnative crops like alfalfa, pecans, citrus, and winter vegetables. (The area around Yuma, for example, now produces much of the nation's winter iceberg lettuce and asparagus crops.) Most of these crops, especially cotton and alfalfa, qualify as agricultural surplus and are subject to several kinds of federal subsidies; and in any event, Mexican citrus and cotton will likely drive Arizona's off the market should the promised North American Free Trade Agreement become a reality. But federal largesse has prompted a great number of landowners to farm despite the obvious effects on the river. Charles Keating, notorious for his role in the savings-and-loan debacle of the late 1980s, planted a bit of barley on his vast Scottsdale estate to qualify as a farmer, and he received a number of tax breaks for his troubles. For years Kemper Marley, a prominent developer, raised a pair of goats on twelve square miles of suburban Phoenix property. His status as a livestock producer saved him $375,000 in taxes every year.

The profligacy of industrial agriculture had other effects on the land, among them the loss of native riparian plants. (One standard irrigation textbook maintains, these "have little or no economic value, and they consume water which normally could be used beneficially for

Advertisements like this promising image lured farmers into the Salt River valley in the early years of the twentieth century. Most of them failed. (Illustration courtesy of the Tucson Public Library)

agricultural and industrial purposes.") In the late nineteenth century, California farmers imported the tamarisk or salt cedar (*Tamarix chinensis*), a weedlike tree, from the Eurasian steppes to aid in erosion control. Within a few years the tree had spread along the banks of the lower Gila, driving out its native counterpart, the seep willow (*Baccharis glutinosa*); today tamarisk occupies the very headwaters of the river. Another introduced plant, cheatgrass (*Bromus tectroum*) has similarly displaced the native bunchgrasses of the Gila basin, which were far more efficient in providing groundcover that aided the soil in retaining moisture.

Still another introduced plant, this one by accident, has come to define the West. The Russian thistle (*Salsola kali*), or tumbleweed, hitched a ride to the United States with Volga German immigrants fleeing Russia in the 1870s; its seeds lay buried amid wheat stock that the immigrants had brought along with them, and it sprang up throughout the Dakotas, where the Volga Germans settled. Within two decades the plant had spread across the West, thriving—as do so many weed species—on the abundant patches of disturbed soil from which native plants had been stripped.

Farming changed the landscape. So did the introduction of large-scale cattle ranching to the Southwest. Cattle had roamed the arid lands of New Spain since the 1500s, filling the ecological niche left by long-extinct Pleistocene browsers like mastodons, horses, and camels, but always in relatively small numbers; the surviving, half-feral criollo herd that attacked the Mormon Battalion numbered no more than a few hundred animals, and the largest Spanish ranch, the size of Massachusetts, supported no more than a hundred thousand cattle and another fifteen thousand horses and mules. With the American conquest of the Southwest and the eventual destruction of Apache power, however, came a different notion, fueled by the nineteenth-century ideology of material progress whose chief assumption was that the world's resources could not be exhausted. The American variation in particular offered the idea that the continent was supernaturally endowed and that conservation was unnecessary, that God would provide eternally for producer and capitalist alike.

A staunch adherent to this belief was Sylvester Mowry, an entrepreneur and booster who had tried without success to have the Gila basin annexed into the Confederacy. He fled to Mexico when the Union reclaimed the region, returned to Tucson in 1873, and set about urging Texas cattlemen to leave the shortgrass prairies for the new promised land. He had a flair for invention, promising his would-be clients that "the sun never shone on better grazing country. . . . The traveler has before him a sea of grass. . . . The stockraiser in January sees his cattle in better condition than our eastern farmer his stall fed ox." When Mowry first came to the Southwest this may have been the case, but between 1850 and 1860 half a million sheep had been driven along the Gila Trail to California to feed the forty-niners, and these hooved locusts had already shaved off much of the groundcover in their path.

No matter. In 1870 there were no more than five thousand head of cattle in the Arizona Territory; two years later that number quadrupled when Henry Hooker quit his Texas ranch and established a new spread along the San Simon, an eastern tributary of the Gila. (One of Hooker's earliest employees was young William McCarty, soon to be known as Billy the Kid.) By 1891, when several other Texans had moved their herds to points up and down the Gila, there were at least 1.5 million cattle in the region, with their numbers growing daily. The 1880s and early 1890s were a good time to be in the beef industry: Europeans, enjoying a newly booming economy owing in large part to the conquest of Africa, were then eating huge quantities of American and Argentine beef, and they provided a seemingly insatiable market.

That market brought a flood of money into the Southwest, a welcome change from the extractive, colonial economies of the East Coast mining interests that had hitherto dominated the region. Eager to increase the flow, in 1883 territorial governor F. A. Tritle claimed that Arizona could sustain 7,680,000 cattle. That number was never reached, but the cattle population of the Gila basin must have numbered nearly three million by the early 1890s.

The effect on the landscape was devastating. Huge herds of cattle roamed across the open range, devouring nearly every plant in their path, shunning only the prickly pear and poisonous lupines—plants that flourish today throughout the Gila basin. The paths that the herds cut into the fragile ground opened up with constant use and rainstorms to form great arroyos, or ravines, that diverted water from natural courses. Within the space of a few years the formerly lush grasslands that bordered the river had been gnawed to the ground by herds of introduced Jersey, Guernsey, Charolais, and longhorn cattle—eating machines that rival sharks for their voracity. The man who introduced longhorns to the Southwest, a forester and former Apache fighter named Will Barnes, later confessed in his memoirs, "We fondly imagined that these wonderful ranges would last forever and couldn't be overstocked." Another rancher, C. H. Bayless, who ran herds along the middle San Pedro, echoed Barnes: "Vegetation does not thrive as it once did . . . because the seed is gone, the roots are gone, and the soil is gone. This is all the direct result of overstocking and cannot be prevented on open range where the land is not subject to private control."

Cattle and the pecuniary promise they brought changed the tenor of the West as well. The Indian nations had been subdued—in General Phil Sheridan's words, so that the West could "be covered with speckled cattle and the festive cowboy"—and for a brief moment in the 1880s it seemed as if peace might finally come to the Gila. But the

Once-fertile grassland along the middle Gila, near Florence, after overgrazing. The land will require generations to recover.
(Photograph by Lynn Jacobs)

conflicting interests of miners, ranchers, farmers, and townspeople quickly erased that hope. Large ranches like the Aztec Land and Cattle Company of northern Arizona, with a spread of more than a million acres and grazing rights along most of the middle Gila, took to hiring cowboys who were more proficient with guns than branding irons, and a range war soon erupted across the Southwest. The Aztec's cowboys terrorized Mormon settlers along the Mogollon Rim, yielding the few ghost towns to exist in the Kingdom of the Latter-Day Saints. Rival cattle companies waged war against each other, leading to inter-family vendettas that rivaled the Hatfield-McCoy feud. When a cohort of Basque immigrants introduced sheep into the Blue River valley at the end of the nineteenth century, both men and animals were massacred, prompting succeeding Basque migrants to establish themselves in less populous Nevada. Towns of the Gila basin became charnel houses in which, as Apache fighter John Cremony observed, "men walked the streets with double-barreled shotguns and hunted each other as sportsmen hunt for game." The time was so violent at home and abroad that Mark Twain proposed changing the stars in the U.S. flag to skulls and crossbones.

Small farmers, too, fell victim to ranching enterprises, for the ranchers required ready access to water for their herds, water that now flowed in *acequias* to the small fields of corn and wheat that dotted the Southwest's river valleys. Some farmers were more than glad to sell out, but others had to be persuaded by force. The obituary columns of newspapers like the *Tombstone Telegraph* and *Silver City Independent* mushroomed as the ranching interests, in Bernard De Voto's words, "did their utmost to keep the nester—the farmer, the actual settler, the man who could create local and permanent wealth—out of the West and to terrorize or bankrupt him where he could not be kept out."

Nature has always provided the deserts with defense mechanisms against the vanity of human wishes, however. Apart from the occasional simoon and cyclical flood, the most powerful has been drought, and drought was what nature visited upon the Gila basin in 1892. O'odham shamans had foretold the disaster two decades earlier, when a massive earthquake in Sonora rumbled throughout the Papaguería, with aftershocks lasting ten seconds and more; they prophesied that I'itoi, the creator, was about to change the face of the earth. Finding in the earthquake a convenient excuse, cattlemen would later claim that it indeed produced the great drought of the 1890s.

The drought settled in for a full decade. The year 1892 was perhaps the worst; out of the already denuded landscape no new grasses sprang forth, and unacclimated English breeds like Devons and Alderneys quickly fell prey to exhaustion, hunger, and thirst. Within a year the hardier Sonoran and Texan cattle joined them, and, as a rancher later reminisced, a person could "actually throw a rock from one carcass to another" across the length of southern New Mexico and Arizona. The rancher did not exaggerate; within three years some two million cattle had died, more than half of the aggregate herds. Men and women died, too, and cowboys were reduced to straining what little water they could find through cheesecloth and burlap in order to filter out the one creature that thrived at the time, the maggots that sprang from rotting corpses.

The drought spread eastward. In the 1890s the population of Kansas fell by half as settlers returned to the East, their wagons bearing the bitter motto, "In God we trusted, in Kansas we busted." Much of Nebraska and the Dakotas was depopulated as the prairies dried up and blew away in the arid winds. The abrupt drop in foreign beef sales helped touch off the great economic Panic of 1893, and in time much of the capitalist world was engulfed in a crisis partly caused, in the end, by three million ravenous cows and the few men who ran them across the grasslands of the Southwest.

In time the summer rains returned, and with them the ranchers. By 1905 they were conducting their business as if the great die-off of 1892 had never occurred. A government report warned them of the consequences of their behavior, prophesying "the total destruction of the grass roots by overstocking. . . . If the herds are not reduced for a sufficient time to allow restocking with grass the [Gila drainage] area will be ruined as grazing land."

But the cattlemen did not listen. Their herds increased year by year, especially after the Mexican Revolution began in 1910 and Sonoran and Chihuahuan ranchers drove half a million head of cattle to safety across the international border. When the grasses failed to spring back in their former abundance, the cattlemen of the Gila basin set about slaughtering the creatures they believed were responsible for the destruction: cottontails and jackrabbits, badgers and marmots, prairie dogs and muledeer. And when that massacre did not yield a verdant grassland, the ranchers brought in consultants like the InterState Artificial Rain Company, whose representatives traveled the West firing skyrockets into the air, pouring mysterious powders onto the ground and taking large sums of money for their services, surely hoping all the while that drenching rains would somehow fall and spare them an application of tar and feathers.

That cows should have become a substantial part of the Southwestern economy is a matter of effective marketing and lobbying. Even in its heyday, the Western cattle industry provided only a small portion of the nation's beef production, and almost no dairy; today, the entire West yields only 2 or 3 percent of the country's beef supply. The reasons are obvious enough: in Alabama, a water-rich beef producer, a cow requires three acres of grazing land for sufficient annual forage, whereas in the West beyond the hundredth meridian the average is two hundred acres. No matter where they are raised, cattle consume nearly three thousand gallons of water for every pound of beef they yield; the available water supplies in the West are simply insufficient to generate beef production at any meaningful level. Yet, as writers like the late Edward Abbey and Len Jacobs have observed, we associate the West with the image of the cowboy, the rugged individualist tending his herds faithfully against the predations of man and beast. That romantic view has for more than a century impeded our view of the cow, and secondarily the sheep, as the arid regions' worst natural enemies.

The Western cattle industry continues to play on that earlier romanticism, appealing to the supposed libertarian ideals of freedom and individual initiative while in fact relying on the largesse of the federal government, without which its production would be unprofitable. Seventy million cattle and eight million sheep graze on 40 percent of all the public lands in the West—that is, properties in the public domain, belonging to you and me and our progeny. The chief beneficiaries are a grand total of some thirty thousand ranching families in the entire West, most of whose livelihoods result directly from government subsidies. Perhaps eight hundred of these families live along the Gila, and they produce a scant .1 percent of the nation's beef supply. (Among their number in the 1950s was the actor John Wayne, who owned the Red River Cattle Company near Casa Grande. It was then the largest private feedlot in the United States.)

The subsidies are staggering. For instance, as of 1993 Western ranchers were paying $1.94 per "animal unit month," or the amount of forage one cow and a calf required for thirty days, in exchange for grazing rights on public lands. That fee is about 20 percent of what it would cost to raise the same cow and calf on private land leased for the purpose. Given the disparity in operating costs, no rancher concerned with realizing a year-end profit can afford to overlook the government's generous handout. (One ranch family along the Gila decided to press for even more. In 1992, the Klumps of Bowie padlocked the gates leading into 87,000 acres of public land bordering the Peloncillo Wilderness near the upper Gila, proclaiming the land to be theirs by virtue of long-term use. As of mid-1993 the case had not been settled.) The inevitable result, as the federal Bureau of Land Management reported in 1975 and again in 1988, is that more than four-fifths of public-domain grazing lands were then in fair or poor condition. The report spurred Congress to pass the Federal Land Policy Management Act of 1976 and the Public Rangeland Improvement Act of 1978, both of which were intended to reduce the number of cattle grazing under any federal aegis in the West. Instead, both acts helped trigger the so-called Sagebrush Rebellion, which was instigated by the livestock industry and which called for federal lands to be turned over to individual states. Under the presidency of Ronald Reagan, who was sympathetic to the "rebels," both pieces of forward-looking legislation were effectively neutered.

During the same period half of all public grazing lands fell under the control, through leasing, of fewer than five hundred individuals and corporations, a spectacular example of trickle-down economics at work. Among the largest shareholders, according to a 1992 Government Accounting Office report, were Hewlett-Packard, Laurence Rockefeller, Aetna, Metropolitan Life, Texaco, and John Hancock, giants all, while a single unnamed Californian had gained grazing rights on more than seven million acres. On reading this report, a conservative Democrat from Oklahoma, Representative Mike Synar, thundered, "It's time we gave [the leaseholders] a good dose of free enterprise."

As one consequence of misgovernment, cattle grazing on Western public lands is now at an all-time high of nearly eleven million head. (At the same time, in the last twenty years per capita beef consumption in the developed nations has fallen by more than a quarter. In the United States, the figure stands at about sixty pounds per person annually.) In 1992, about 800,000 of these cattle grazed on public lands in Arizona, yielding fewer than five thousand jobs and about $43 million in revenue, an economic contribution far behind that of, say, convenience stores and air-conditioning repair shops; the figures are about the same for New Mexico. Like other extractive enterprises in the West, in other words, ranching is strictly a marginal endeavor.

The environmental effects are incommensurate. The few permanent streams in the Southwest have been permanently degraded, their banks collapsed by the weight of passing cattle, their waters impurified by defecation to the point that even the remotest branch carries the threat of *Giardia lamblia* and other waterborne bacteria that spread disease. A third of the Southwest's grazing land is now severely desertified, and throughout the West some 685 million acres of public lands are threatened by the same fate: once-rich soils, loosened in the absence of adequate native grasses, turn into dust that blows across the sere landscape, now denuded of trees. The 1930s and 1940s offered a harbinger of what would follow the desertification of the land, as John Steinbeck recorded in *The Grapes of Wrath*:

> *When the night came again it was black night, for the stars could not pierce the dust to get down, and the window lights could not even spread beyond their own yards. . . . Houses were shut tight, and cloth wedged around doors and windows, but the dust came in so thinly that it could not be seen in the air, and it settled like pollen on the chairs and tables, on the dishes. The people brushed it from their shoulders. Little lines of dust lay at the door sills.*

The Dust Bowl took in a vast swath of land, including much of southern New Mexico, but it affected areas far beyond its immediate compass. Twelve million tons of plains dust drifted through downtown Chicago doors on May 10, 1934, for instance, and a few days later the same storm deposited dust under the door of the White House. The apocalypse sent more than 300,000 residents of the Great Plains reeling to California between 1935 and 1939. Far fewer settled in the vicinity of the Gila, in odd corners of the land like Pie Town, New Mexico, and Mohawk, Arizona, but their numbers presaged the postwar boom that sent the population of Phoenix, Los Angeles, and other Western towns skyrocketing.

"Soil," the great conservationist Aldo Leopold noted, "is the fundamental resource, and its loss the most serious of all losses." The conditions leading to the Dust Bowl pale by comparison with the destruction of the land over the last half-century, because of which the western states are undergoing desertification at a rate at least twice as fast as the Sahel, the driest region of arid Africa. Yet the delusions continue. When the president of the Arizona Cattleman's Association averred in 1992, "our range lands are in the best shape now that they've ever been in," few voices rose in opposition. And a corral now suffocates what once was a garden.

Cattle were not alone in reshaping the Gila during the West's boom years. In the 1860s the federal government granted railroad companies huge tracts of land throughout the West as rights of way, with the understanding that the railroads could then profitably extend their lines into the newly conquered territories. These rights of way comprised two hundred feet of land on either side of the track plus any and all land the railroads deemed necessary for yards, stations, and sidings. (Not surprisingly, many railroads determined that they needed a lot of ground for such things.) In addition, every alternate section of public land on each side of the tracks was also ceded, and unlimited access to publicly owned forests was granted. The growth of the railroads coincided with the late-nineteenth-century Southwestern mining boom, which similarly ate up huge swaths of forest. Geographer Conrad Bahre has calculated that one mine alone, the Tombstone Bonanza on the middle San Pedro, consumed eighty thousand cords of mesquite, juniper, and oak from 1879 to 1886, burned for fuel for the stamp mills. And this small mine was but one of thousands that lined the Gila.

Within a few decades the great virgin woodlands of the West had been stripped bare, including huge stands of ponderosa pine at the headwaters of the Gila and along the Mogollon Rim; by 1920 more than 80 percent of these primeval woodlands had been clearcut, and from 1970 to the present alone more than a million acres of old-growth forest have been destroyed forever. If you travel across this area today, you will note the significant absence of "yellow pines"—

The Contention Mill, near Tombstone, Arizona. The huge stacks of
mesquite cordwood are sufficient to fuel the mill for a few hours at best.
(Photograph courtesy of the Bancroft Library)

light-hued ponderosas that are more than a hundred years old—and
the proliferation of "blackjacks"—dark-hued young trees that grow in
suspiciously neat rows. The large trees are gone, milled after World
War II to provide timber for the housing boom and, in later years, to
fuel the seemingly insatiable desires of resource-poor industrial nations
like Japan, which is now pouring massive amounts of money into
developing the newly opened Siberian hardwood forests, logged
at a rate of 10 million acres annually. You will also note few signs
of a healthy forest: understory growth, moss, decaying logs, and
"snags," standing dead trees that provide indispensable wildlife
habitats. In the national forests such untidy assemblages are
cleared away, and the earth surrounding the neatly planted trees
has all the personality of a suburban lawn.

The woodlands of the West early on came under the jurisdiction of the federal government. In 1907, President Theodore Roosevelt mandated the creation of the U.S. Forest Service and appointed Gifford Pinchot its first director. Pinchot was no preservationist. "The National Forests," he remarked in one of his first pieces of official correspondence, "will always be of value chiefly for the production of timber and wood." Pinchot formulated a two-horned policy of "sustainable yield" and "multiple use" for the forests under his charge, which translated into a doctrine that the Forest Service continues to observe today: like other public lands, the national forests are regarded as areas of production, natural factories from which to derive maximum profit.

In 1662, when the Puritan seminarian Michael Wigglesworth called the forests of America "a waste & howling wilderness where none inhabit but hellish fiends & brutish men," the area of the present continental United States contained 950 million acres of virgin forest. By 1920 the area had been reduced to 464 million acres, and much of the cutting had been carried out before the eyes of the Forest Service. Pinchot's policies were so damaging that as early as 1936 Interior Secretary Harold Ickes decried their effects. "To the United States Forest Service," he said, "a tree is something to be cut down. . . . The nobler the tree, the greater the desire to see it laid low. . . . No tree that has reached maturity, even if its majesty and beauty would endure for a thousand years, could escape a sentence of death if the Forest Service had its way." Ickes properly observed that Pinchot's doctrine of multiple use really meant "use up."

To no avail. The advent of the Second World War brought with it a frenzy of war production and the suspension of such modest conservation measures as had been taken, and in 1943 a Forest Service pamphlet could comfortably proclaim the resurrection of Pinchot's policies: "We tame our forests so that we will get better service from them, domesticate them as we have domesticated horses, wheat, cabbages and hens." The Forest Service authorized massive clearcutting throughout the 168 million acres of woodlands under its control. Forty years ago each citizen of the United States owned twenty trees on the nation's public lands. Now each of us owns four.

In the last hundred years, Arizona's national forests—almost all of them within the Gila drainage—have been more intensively cut than have the trees of any other Western state. One percent of the state's total reserve of eight thousand square miles is now logged each year, yielding about 350 million board feet of timber annually; under the guidance of Interior Secretary James Watt, the Reagan administration briefly boosted this production to 500 million board feet. New Mexico's national forests have fared no better.

But once again, these economic activities are at best marginal. In the last decade the Forest Service timber program has lost $5.6 billion, ninety-five cents on the dollar, in systematic violation of federal law. (Similarly, the Bureau of Land Management recovers only 37 percent of the cost of providing grazing on federal lands.) In 1992 alone the Forest Service spent $600 million to make its holdings accessible to private loggers, and earned only $118 million in return; if all logging in the national forests of Arizona and New Mexico were to be suspended tomorrow, the economic loss would amount to only $20 million and 3,100 jobs.

Robert Penn Warren has written, "the machine defines the act." The Ancient Mariner shot the albatross because he had a crossbow. We clearcut our national forests because we have the drag chains and giant saws that enable us to do it. At an incalculable cost, a quarter of the world's timber comes from the United States. Lacking anchorage in the roots of mature trees, understory shrubs, and bunchgrasses, the topsoils of our logged highlands wash into the rivers of America and on into the seas, a loss of our most vital natural resource.

The steamboat Cocopah *at Yuma, ca. 1890. By that time most of the Gila was nonnavigable.* (Photograph courtesy of the Arizona Historical Society)

When Anglo Americans first came to the Southwest, much of the Gila River was navigable. Within half a century it no longer carried enough water to float a raft. For newcomers who had read of the abundant waters of the desert, this was a constant source of confusion. One of them was a government inspector charged with Indian affairs who came to the Arizona Territory in the late 1880s, bearing an official map that showed the Gila as a live river. He asked at Yuma when the next boat would sail for the Pima Villages and was told, "Well, when the Gila gets water, we'll be sure to get a line of boats running for your convenience." The inspector produced his map and declared that the surveyors of the government could not possibly be wrong. Eventually, frustrated by his interlocutor's refusal to admit that the river carried water, he took a stagecoach. At the stage stop at Maricopa Wells he related the story to the driver, who told him, "You must have fallen in with a damned lot of liars working in the interest of the stagecoach line. The Gila is navigable. A boat leaves Yuma every day for the Pima villages. Look yonder: there's one now!" He pointed to a column of whirling, smokelike dust a few miles distant. The inspector grabbed his bags and went off. An hour later the driver wandered into a saloon and bragged about his prank, and a samaritan went out and retrieved the inspector, who had fainted of thirst in the parched desert.

The lesson to be drawn: in the desert, do not put your faith in maps. Two days before Christmas in 1944, twenty-five German sailors who had been interned as prisoners of war in a makeshift camp within Papago Park, an area of Phoenix on the banks of the Salt River, tunneled out with the intention of stealing a boat and then sailing down the Gila and Colorado to Mexico. They too carried maps that showed the Gila to be a perennial river, but when they reached its banks and saw but a pitiful trickle of water, they abandoned their plan and set downriver on foot. Within two days most of them were rounded up and returned to the prison camp.

Their leader, Captain Wolfgang Clarus, later complained, "I only wish the Gila really had been a river. If it has no water, why do the Americans show it on their maps?"

The time will come when they will sell
you even your own rain.
—Thomas Merton

8

DISAPPEARED
WATERS

The climate of the American Southwest, noted John Graves in his requiem for the Brazos, *Goodbye to a River*, "accords ill with the Saxon nostalgia for cool, green, dew-wet landscapes." Nonetheless, the children of northern Europe have been making their way to these dry places in increasing numbers for a century and a half, bringing their nostalgia with them. As a rule, they have not been good about adapting to the sere landscape. They remember as eccentrics those who have, like Edward Fitzgerald Beale, who advocated the formation of an army camel corps to patrol the deserts. In order to recapture something of the green past, these newcomers enslaved the free-flowing rivers of the West, even killing some in their zeal.

But they still knew, despite their dreams of Europe, that water was a resource to be guarded jealously. (An anthropologist once asked a Hopi why so many of his people's songs were about rain. The Hopi replied that it was because water is so scarce; is that why so many of your songs are about love?) The problem was somehow to conquer water so that it could be used at leisure. The Southwest's boosters lost no time in turning eastward to Washington to demand that this conquest be put into motion. One of them, A. J. Chandler, for whom the Arizona town along the Gila is named, had gone to Europe in 1893 to try to raise capital for a dam to span the twin buttes above Florence, and another on the site of present Roosevelt Dam. When his pleas were denied, owing to worldwide economic depression, Chandler set about lobbying politicians everywhere for legislation that would make the prosperous settlement of the Gila basin Washington's business.

One of the men most willing to listen to Chandler was Theodore Roosevelt. In his first address to Congress in 1901, Roosevelt set forth Chandler's argument:

> *Vast areas of public land can be made available for homestead settlement, but only by reservoirs and mainline canals impracticable for private enterprise. These irrigation works should be built by the national government. The lands reclaimed by them should be reserved by the government for actual settlers, and the cost of construction should be, so far as is possible, repaid by the land reclaimed.*

The result of his importuning was the National Reclamation Act of 1902, by which the nation would indeed pay for massive water projects and, in theory, be reimbursed by those who benefited from the government's aid. Western states and territories hurried to claim their share of the federal reclamation budget, and powerful California took most of it. Arizona received authorization for a dam on the Salt River, completed in 1911, its lobbyists having wisely decided to name it after the president; but only a decade later would significant funding come to Arizona and New Mexico.

In the meanwhile, the Gila made its own cases. In February 1904 the river flooded as a result of an early snowmelt coupled with unusually heavy winter rains, swamping many towns along its banks. The discharge spilled into the Colorado, itself swollen, carrying along with it a huge uprooted oak tree. The tree broke through a control gate above Yuma, sending a torrent of water into the old bed of the long-dead Alamo River, and within a year the flood had carved a new course to its ancient terminus in the Salton Sink of south-central California— now, with the reappearance of water after thousands of years, called the Salton Sea. The flooding was even more spectacular in 1905. During flood periods desert rivers can carry a sediment load of 75 percent of their total volume (in one day of flooding in October 1941 the San Juan River at Mexican Hat, Utah, carried twelve million tons of sediment, thirty-five times the annual load of the entire Mississippi at St. Paul), and the Gila in 1905 ground its way out of hundreds of the check dams and through the embankments that had been constructed along its course.

Such wild behavior would not be tolerated. In 1912 a Los Angeles developer, Joseph Lippincott, demanded that the rivers of the West be reined in to feed his city. Mindful of engineering feats half a world away that had been filling the news, he proclaimed the Colorado River system to be the "Nile of America," and, like Chandler, he set about converting politicians to his cause. Californians had special reason to be interested, for to shackle the Colorado meant a well-watered Central Valley and a Southland that could be made ripe for development. At the same time, diverting water from the Colorado above the international boundary meant keeping it from the Chinese and Japanese farmers who had settled below it, in the vicinity of Mexicali, and who were fast developing northern Mexico's agricultural base. Lippincott and others were able to use the rhetoric of "yellow peril" to advantage.

Ten years of negotiations ensued before the Western states in the

Colorado basin—Wyoming, Utah, Colorado, New Mexico, Arizona, Nevada, and California—were able to come to an accord on how the river should be divided up. Their compact of 1922 assumed that the main river carried an annual flow of 16 million acre feet, about half of which was to be allocated to the upper-basin states. It soon developed that the Colorado normally carried only 14 million acre feet, but the upper-basin states refused to renegotiate their allotment, leaving the lower-basin states to slug it out for themselves. They did for the next fifty years, a seemingly endless series of episodes in the legacy of conflict that John Wesley Powell foresaw. The battle devolved into a series of lawsuits, one of which ended up before the U.S. Supreme Court as one of the most complicated cases in its history. In 1966, the weary judges awarded Arizona an allotment of 2.8 million acre feet, a million of which was to come from the Gila. This was more than Arizona had expected, and was adequate to irrigate the three million acres of farmland that lay along the Gila's course.

Arizona's senior senator, Carl Hayden, who served in Congress for half a century, had long lobbied for the allotment, and for massive public-works projects to see that it was delivered to his constituency. In 1968 his efforts were rewarded by the passage of the Colorado River Basin Project Act, authorizing the construction of a series of dams and a 335-mile-long canal that would divert water from the Colorado near its junction with the Bill Williams River, taking it through Phoenix and on to Tucson.

Four decades earlier, thanks again to Hayden's efforts, the first major impediment on the Gila, Coolidge Dam, rose at the opening of what Lieutenant William Emory called "a savage box canyon" on the western edge of the San Carlos Apache Reservation. Completed in 1930 during one of the region's periodic dry cycles, the dam created a vast reservoir that filled in so slowly that when Will Rogers dedicated the dam he remarked, "If this was my lake, I'd mow it." An elderly

Coolidge Dam under construction in the late 1920s. (Photograph courtesy of the Arizona Historical Society)

Apache man recalls that, for his part, the dam's namesake, former president Calvin Coolidge, was so afraid of the Indians who had gathered to hear the celebratory speeches that he refused to step outside the train that had brought him to the site, instead speaking only for a moment from the vestibule. He might have had reason to be afraid, for one of the effects of the dam was to flood the best farmland in the area, causing a temporary famine throughout the Apache nation.

Equipped for hydroelectric power generation, but never used for the purpose, Coolidge Dam soon demonstrated a fact of life about desert rivers: they carry vast quantities of sand and rock, all the more so in the case of the Gila because of the depletion of topsoils through agricultural malpractice. Hydrologists have called the Gila the muddiest river in the world. The San Carlos Reservoir began silting up almost instantly; in 1930 it held 1,266,837 acre feet of water, which dropped to 1,170,000 acre feet in 1966 and to less than a million acre

Coolidge Dam after flooding in the winter of 1992. The reservoir is nearly full to capacity. (Photograph by the author)

feet today. Still, it had its effects, and the Gila River stopped flowing west of the so-called Copper Basin of central Arizona after 1940. The bone-dry channel could have carried a small sea; because of erosion the streambed of the Gila near the Pima Villages, formerly two hundred feet in width, was nearly two thousand feet wide by 1945. Similarly, the channel of the San Pedro near its confluence with the Gila was about ten feet deep in 1870. Forty years later it stood at nearly eighty feet deep. Farmers at Safford reported the loss of an astonishing 1,100 acres of topsoil in 1915, prompting H. R. Love, an officer of the U.S. Soil Conservation Service, to propose that a network of 75,000 check dams be erected along the river.

Frank H. Olmstead, a federal geologist who surveyed the Gila in 1915 to report on the feasibility of dams, agreed. He presciently remarked on the consequences of the national mania for altering rivers:

> It is true that we are a new country and have been so preoccupied in the subjugation of the land to the uses of man that perhaps up to this time we may be pardoned for not more acutely realizing the waste and danger associated with our compelled interference with nature's control of the streams and our failure to initiate compensating tendencies restraining them. It has both been stated and denied by recognized authorities that floods over the earth are increasing, and that the same physical penalties which overtook the Assyrians and the Babylonians on the fertile plains of the Tigris and the Euphrates are steadily advancing in their inexorable conquest of the lowlands of this country.

Olmstead, too, advocated building many check dams rather than large structures, arguing that the resulting saturation of the surrounding soil would enable "nature to recover herself from the spoliation of the forces of waste and to build up again the fern and willow growth and to recreate the moisture-filled soil storage that all through the dry season should be furnishing its little quota of flow to the river below." But such check dams lacked the glamour and pork-barrel potential of the huge structures that prevailed, and Olmstead's observations went largely unnoticed until modern times.

Apart from the devastation it caused the riverine environment, Coolidge Dam was notoriously mismanaged for years by the always inept Bureau of Indian Affairs (BIA). When the Gila flooded in October 1983 after a series of powerful El Niño-system storms, the BIA discovered that the dam's floodgates were inoperable, having been rusted shut at least a decade earlier; none of the dam operators seems to have noticed. That year the Government Accounting Office rated Coolidge the most dangerous dam in the country—if you stand on the causeway, hundreds of feet above the riverbed, you'll notice that the dam's outer piers are beginning to separate from its main body. The BIA seemed content not to do anything for a decade, after which it was awarded $11.5 million to stabilize the dam by covering the canyon walls alongside it with concrete two and a half feet thick to "prevent erosion" and by rebuilding the spillways to accommodate larger volumes of water releases.

Coolidge is foremost among several dams in the Gila basin that are in trouble. Of the eleven that now control runoff from the Mogollon Rim—Bartlett and Horseshoe on the Verde; Roosevelt, Horse Mesa, Mormon Flat, Stewart Mountain, and Granite Reef on the Salt; and Coolidge, Hayden-Ashurst, Gillespie, and Painted Rock directly on the Gila—nearly half have been faulted for poor construction, and several have undergone major renovation.

The dam builders want more. The 1968 legislation approving the Central Arizona Project (CAP) authorizes a dam at the site A. J. Chandler had proposed the century before, intended to impound the scant 75,000 acre feet that flows off from the San Pedro into the Gila; Buttes

Dam has not been built, although there are occasional noises about it. A second impediment, Hooker Dam, would have backed up six miles into the Gila Wilderness at the headwaters of the river. This dam, unnecessary by any measure, was authorized as a sop to New Mexico, so that its legislators would vote in favor of Arizona during the original debates on the CAP as long as New Mexico could take 50,000 acre feet from the Gila. (A later Bureau of Reclamation study determined, though, that it would take two dams on the upper Gila to salvage just 35,000 acre feet.) A *New York Times* editorial of 1968 denounced Hooker Dam, but the CAP still passed with it intact, and dam builders were set to go to work on it until residents of Silver City and other headwaters towns organized to protest its construction, waging a highly effective campaign of citizen action. After that defeat the Bureau of Reclamation looked for an alternative site downriver; if a dam is built there, the bird sanctuary near Red Rock, New Mexico, would be drowned. Still, both Butte and Hooker remain on the authorized roll, and they may yet be constructed.

Now a great canal, visible from the moon to the naked eye, snakes across the Arizona desert, bringing water from one overallocated river system into the compass of another. It does few of the things that flowing waters are supposed to do: the canal, fenced along much of its course, provides no refuge for wildlife, no suitable environment for riparian vegetation. Yet it suits the aims of the developers who have pushed for its creation over decades, for it allows Arizona (and New Mexico, by making possible a larger allotment from the Gila) to grow and grow, illustrating Edward Abbey's observation, "Growth for its own sake is the ideology of the cancer cell."

The canal is also a spectacular example of waste. Nearly 40 percent of its water load is lost to evaporation in the desert sun (when it comes down to it, laying an underground pipeline would have made more sense); another 30 percent is lost in climbing the twelve hundred ver-

The take-in point for the Los Angeles Aqueduct above the confluence of the Bill Williams and Colorado rivers. Water projects pockmark the watercourses of the West. (Photograph by the author)

tical feet from the Colorado River to Phoenix and the additional thousand feet to Tucson. (But, as a Western adage puts it, "water flows uphill toward money.") Moreover, when the final bill for its construction arrives, the taxpayers of the United States will face payment of $3.6 billion. By the rules of the Reclamation Act of 1902, those who benefit from an irrigation project are meant to pay for it; but in the case of the CAP, consumers of electricity locally and taxpayers nationwide will provide the means by which a resident of Phoenix will pay, on average, four times less for water than will a resident of New York City, that water-rich chimera to the east. That Phoenician, incidentally, will use three hundred gallons of water daily, the highest rate of consumption in the nation.

At the turn of the twentieth century, the Southwestern writer

Mary Austin noted, "Rain falls on radical and conservative alike, but the mother ditch makes communists of them all." Fifty years later the late historian and novelist Wallace Stegner would add, in a neat twist on Karl Wittfogel's hypothesis, that the origins of the modern welfare state are to be found in the federal government's management of the Western public domain. The CAP offers a powerful argument in Stegner's favor. But the final irony is that now that the CAP is finished, the recipients of the central government's handouts—the farmers and ranchers in whose interest it was built—do not want the salt-laden water it brings. The direct cost of the canal to the government is about $80 per acre foot; in turn, it has for many years been requiring farmers to pay only $3.50. In 1990 talk came of raising the ante to $50—a figure still wildly below the so-called market value of the water—but the agricultural and ranching lobbies balked, urging that those of their constituents who had taken of the great canal return to their deep-well turbine pumps and continue to raise their crops and beasts on the fossil groundwater whose depletion the CAP was meant to forestall. Arizona farmers did not start paying for groundwater at all until 1984, and they now pay but a dollar an acre foot; New Mexico farmers enjoyed much the same privilege.

The evidence of this "tragedy of the commons" now pockmarks the Southwest. In the last thirty years, groundwater levels have dropped by eighty feet even in the most distant rural areas. The current overdrafting of groundwater—that is, its rate of removal from the soil vis-à-vis its recharge—in Arizona is 2.2 million acre feet annually, and the water table below Tucson, which lay a hundred years ago nearly at the surface, has dropped a hundred meters, roughly the length of a football field. The land is laced with sinkholes and collapsed roadways, with human-induced geologic faults that did not exist when the hidden waters were left safe.

Lacking a permanent supply of free or near-free water, many

Southwestern farmers are abandoning their fields in any event. They have found willing buyers for their spreads, not among other farmers but among municipalities. Over the last two decades Phoenix has acquired half a million acres of land throughout western Arizona—drive a hundred and fifty miles west of the metropolis and you'll see the yucca-studded desert strewn with street signs, announcing your arrival at 459th Avenue and points west. The city acquired 30,000 acre feet annually from the purchase of a single farm, and "water ranching" has become one of rural Arizona's few growth industries. And for good reason: analysts for the Arizona Department of Planning and Economic Development announced as long ago as 1971 that if all its water went to municipal and industrial use, the state could support a population of twenty million.

In a land of dead rivers and salted fields, we may see such a monstrous development in our lifetime. But we also may not, for justice took at least one turn for the good in the closing years of the Reagan-Bush era of malfeasant government. It involved the rights of Native Americans to water, and its resolution may change the face of the Gila basin.

Indians have long been used to our trail of broken treaties—of 370 signed between the 1780s and 1880s, not a single pact between the federal government and the Indian nations has been preserved in its entirety. The Supreme Court legitimized this dreary legacy of betrayal in its 1903 ruling on *Lone Wolf* vs. *Hitchcock*, declaring that Congress has the right to abrogate treaties unilaterally. In the West, a great many of these broken treaties have had to do with water. The Wyoming Doctrine replaced English common-law riparian rights with prior appropriation; that is, who got to the river first controlled it. However, the Wyoming Doctrine in time gave way to a variant, the Winters Doctrine, which states that Indians on reservations are entitled to all the water they can use. (It has its basis in a Spanish law of 1713, itself based on the Roman Institutes of Justinian: "Indian towns shall be given a site with sufficient water, arable lands, woodland, and access routes so they can cultivate their lands.") The Winters Doctrine was often cited but rarely enforced, and Indian water continued to nourish Anglo fields and sweep aside the mountains that shielded ore from miners' eyes.

In January 1992, however, the Winters Doctrine returned with a vengeance in the form of the Gila River Adjudication, an umbrella suit involving 65,000 individual claims brought by a united front of Indians—Apaches, Akimel O'odham, Yavapais, and Tohono O'odham working in concert for the first time—that claimed two million acre feet, nearly the whole flow of the Gila. The suit was settled in their favor, and the litigants plan to lease water for $1,200 per acre foot, a not unreasonable sum for residential use but prohibitive for the marginal agriculture Arizonans and New Mexicans have favored. The suit may finally drive the producers of water-hungry cotton, alfalfa, asparagus, citrus, and pecans to wetter ground.

But even municipal uses of water have their costs, quite apart from the prospect of twenty million people living where a fifth of that number now reside. Sunbelt municipalities and the retirement communities that ring many of them mean golf courses—a lure that brings in millions of tourist dollars to the states of New Mexico and Arizona each year. Golf courses use anywhere between half a million and a million gallons of water a day in order to keep their greens lush, and for many years those courses south of the Gila were freshened daily with fossil groundwater while the resident population drank treated effluent from nearby sewage plants.

And so, for golf courses and lemon trees and the prospect of millions of latter-day pioneers, dams continue to be built and maintained along the course of the Gila and other Southwestern rivers. (The 1992 federal budget included $18.6 million for Arizona water projects, $16 million for New Mexico.) Out this way, thanks to just such thinking, rivers are an endangered species.

And so are many of the animal and plant species that line them. The assault on the life-forms of the Gila goes on, as the assault on all life continues in these waning days of this millennium. The yield is a Homeric catalog of extinctions: 47 of the 530-odd species now listed under the Endangered Species Act are found along its course.

Merriam's turkey (*Meleagris gallopavo merriami*), the American bittern (*Botaurus lentiginosus*), Abert's towhee (*Pipilo aberti*), the northern goshawk (*Accipiter gentilis*), and other nesters at the headwaters have seen their habitats destroyed by logging. The willow flycatcher (*Empidonax traillii*), once abundant throughout the riparian corridors alongside the river, has been reduced to three or four nesting pairs; the Mexican spotted owl (*Strix occidentalis*), cousin to the northern spotted-owl that drew so much attention to the old-growth forests of Oregon and Washington in the early 1990s, has suffered similarly.

The snowy egret (*Egretta thula*), once abundant along the Gila, was hunted nearly to extinction in the 1910s and 1920s, when Jazz Age fashion designers used its plumes for flapper outfits. The species recovered somewhat when frivolity gave way to the Dust Bowl and the Depression, but they are once again declining in the Southwest as wetlands continue to diminish. And only twenty-eight pairs of bald eagles (*Haliaeetus leucocephalus*), our national symbol, now fly along the Gila. They cannot detect fish in the muddy stream that the repeated damming of the river has produced, and the Gila thus can no longer sustain them.

The mountain lion (*Felis concolor*) has all but disappeared from the highlands of the Gila, along with most of the jaguars (*Pantera onca*), ocelots (*Felis pardalis*), jaguarundis (*Felis yagouaroundi*), and bobcats (*Felis rufus*). Merriam's elk (*Cervus elaphus merriami*), an important source of food for the larger cats, has been extinct since 1906,

At least eleven mountain lions met their deaths in just a few days of
1988 on a riverside ranch in eastern Arizona. They supposedly preyed
on the ranch's cattle and were likely killed instead
by the area's abundant feral dogs.
(Photograph courtesy of Steve Johnson)

and in any event the big cats have been ruthlessly hunted in the name
of livestock protection; Ben Lilly, a turn-of-the-century hunter in the
Gila wilderness at the river's headwaters, killed seven hundred lions
and perhaps five hundred grizzly bears (*Ursus arctos horribilis*) in the
space of a decade, and he was just one of perhaps a hundred professional hunters in the region.

The Mexican gray wolf (*Canis lupus baileyi* and *mogollonensis*) has
been absent from the headwaters of the Gila since 1920. In 1897 a
local rancher wrote to his congressman that the wolves were destroying

half a million head of cattle each year in the Gila highlands—an incredible exaggeration, but one that led the government to establish a program to destroy predators. Stanley Young, a government biologist, put the matter baldly in a letter of 1936: the wolf, he said, "is one hundred percent criminal, killing for sheer blood lust. . . . All wolves are killers." (The conservationist Aldo Leopold countered, "A deer herd deprived of wolves and coyotes is more dangerous to wilderness areas than the most piratical senator or the go-gettingest chamber of commerce.") There are now only forty-four Mexican gray wolves known to be in the United States, all bred in captivity. Similarly, the coyote (*Canis latrans*) has been ruthlessly hunted; in the last seventy years federal agents have killed at least five million, and as many as half a million a year are being killed as I write. It happens that most of the damage to livestock attributed to coyotes and wolves is the work of feral dogs, which are common in rural areas of the Southwest. In 1989, Arizona Animal Defense Control agents killed nine black bears (*Ursus americanus*), a usually gentle and reclusive creature, as well as more than sixteen hundred coyotes and forty-four mountain lions in the presumed interests of making the woodlands safe for cattle.

The Gila monster (*Heloderma suspectum*), its name the vehicle by which many outsiders know the name of the river and a "living fossil" far better adapted to the Southwest's temperate past than to its arid present, is still wantonly killed for sport or for its neurotoxic venom, or captured for commercial roadside zoos. An object of hatred since Spanish times, the unfortunate creature had developed a great body of folklore by the time Anglos came to the region. A traveling reporter overheard a drunken cowboy bragging of his exploits with the Gila monster: "I've seed a lizard what could out-pizen any frog or toad in the world. . . . [My pistol] shot blew the body clean in two, and then I hope to die if the fore-legs didn't get that pistol clean away from me, jump into the [Gila] river and swim away with it." Respond-

Gila monsters have been an object of loathing since the Europeans
first came to the Sonoran Desert. Here a Phoenix woman,
ca. 1900, holds a pair of unlucky reptiles.
(Photograph courtesy of the Arizona Historical Society)

ing in general to such stories, one Phoenix doctor remarked as early
as 1899 that "a man who is foolish enough to get bitten by a Gila
monster ought to die," but that has not kept the mythology from
thriving, to the everlasting hardship of the beaded lizard. The unre-
lated worm lizard (*Bipes biporus*), once reportedly abundant along the
river, has not been seen for years. And the desert tortoise (*Gopherus
agassizi*) may soon be gone as well, its habitats destroyed by the off-
road vehicles and motorcycles that plow mercilessly across the desert
in the quest for cheap thrills.

The saguaro cactus (*Cereus giganteus*), a symbol of Arizona (and,
thanks to slipshod research out Hollywood way, of the entire West)
has been endangered since the 1880s through overgrazing by cattle
of the protective groundcover and its seedlings and pups. Rodents are
fond of young saguaros as well, and their numbers have exploded in
tandem with the overall decline of their natural predators; some biologists predict that large swaths of the once-great saguaro forest, especially near urban areas, will disappear by the year 2000. Cattle and
rodents are not the only threat to the saguaro, which is pollinated by
the white-lined sphinx moth (*Hyles lineata*), a graceful creature that
thrives in irrigated fields. The moths carry pesticides from those fields
to the fruit of the saguaro, and these fruit in turn are aborted. Given
that industrial agriculture's reliance on chemical pesticides and fertil-
izers is ever increasing, the stately saguaro may be in for rough times.

The various kinds of agaves that sustained the indigenes of the
Gila basin for millennia—the historic O'odham once harvested half a
million agaves a year—are under siege, for the bats that pollinate them
are disappearing. In one cave near the San Francisco River, a tributary
of the upper Gila, more than 50 million Mexican freetail bats (*Tad-
arida brasiliensis*) nested in the mid-1960s. Two decades later the
number had fallen to 25,000, owing to extensive agricultural spraying

with new varieties of pesticides, and the agave population is declining along with the bats.

The ironwood tree (*Olneya tesota*), which often lives to be eight hundred years old, is rapidly disappearing. Apart from the gradual destruction of its habitat, it is now being felled for charcoal and the expanding Mexican woodcarving industry.

The cottonwood-willow-mesquite bosques that once lined the river now contain among the most endangered plant species in the world, representing an American Amazonia. (By recent estimates, in fact, a virgin cottonwood-willow-mesquite ecosystem carries roughly the same biomass as an equivalent patch of Amazonian rainforest.) Many of the cotton fields that replaced them have long since been abandoned, but native plants like the wolfberry (*Lycium fremontii*), barrel cactus (*Ferocactus acanthodes*), and creosotebush (*Larrea tridentata*) cannot live in the now salt-encrusted ground. More than 90 percent of Arizona and New Mexico's riparian environments and gallery forests of willow, velvet ash, cottonwood, sycamore, walnut, and hackberry have been destroyed in the last century.

Native crustaceans like the mitten crab (*Pseudothelphuche sonorense*), native fish like the Gila trout (*Salmo gilae*), Gila topminnow (*Poeciliopsis occidentalis*), and the monstrous, thirteen-foot-long humpback sucker (*Xyrauchen texanus*) have disappeared from the river where they once flourished—Lieutenant Manje reported that their numbers were "infinite"—the victims of low water flows and repeated damming. In their place have come exotic species that, for whatever reason, seem to be better adapted to irregular streamflows, fish like the carp and bullhead, which crowd out competing species. Nearly a third of North America's native fish species once swam the rivers of the Southwest; most of those are now extinct in those waters, or sad ciphers on the federal list of endangered species.

Seventeen percent of the extirpations that have taken place in North America since 1600 have occurred in the Southwest. (As the biologist Edward O. Wilson has said, "Eliminate one species, and another increases in number to take its place. Eliminate a great many species, and the whole ecosystem starts to decay visibly.") The extinctions continue, and those who perpetrate them today know full well what they are doing. A recent case in point has taken place in the high mountains above the middle Gila.

Now, from the tallest building in my hometown of Tucson, whenever the dust and automobile exhaust are down, a clear-eyed observer can see four astronomical observatories in as many directions. The oldest, on the campus of the University of Arizona, has been in use since the first years of the twentieth century, before the discovery of the planet Pluto. The others are of more recent vintage: the Mount Lemmon complex north of the city and Kitt Peak National Observatory, near the sacred Baboquívari Mountains to the west, date to the 1960s, while the Mount Hopkins Multiple-Mirror Telescope complex, on the road south to Mexico, opened in 1973, in the days when southern Arizona's night sky blazed with stars now hidden by evidence of our progress.

Beyond the city lie many other observatories. Of southeastern Arizona's dozen major mountain ranges, only a few lack astronomical facilities. For years astronomers from around the world have traveled to Tucson to take their turn at one or another of these observatories—so many that homegrown junior scholars often have difficulty booking time to complete their research projects; the demand for more and more scopes is consequently high. Used to having their way, the astronomers were not prepared to take seriously Arizona congressman Morris Udall's warning, at the dedication of the Mount Hopkins complex, that they allot their resources conservatively. This, he said, would be the last southern Arizona mountaintop to be shaved off in the name of science.

Rather than reduce the number of observers and make do with what was already an embarrassment of riches, the administration of the University of Arizona, determined to safeguard the school's reputation as the "Wall Street of astronomy," turned to the last of the scopeless mountains. It set its sights on the Pinaleño Range a hundred miles east of Tucson, the summit of which, 10,700-foot Mount Graham, seemed an ideal spot for a new observatory, with no city lights to obscure the faint glow of faraway galaxies, few turbulent windstreams, and little humidity in the desert air. Lying within the Coronado National Forest and once a part of the San Carlos Apache Reservation (the Apache name for the range is *Dzil naá chán*, "Big Seated Mountain"), the range had been hunted, logged, mined, and grazed—for such is the inevitable fate of land in the public domain— and a network of roads led nearly to its top. The job of subduing the mountain had been under way for decades, and it would be a simple enough matter to divert a few million dollars of the university's operating budget in order to build a modern highway, clearcut the old-growth spruce and fir forest, and wrest away the secrets of the firmament.

But, the university learned, matters were more complicated than that. In the early 1980s, Udall, then the chairman of the House Interior Committee, saw to it that the Pinaleños were included in the Arizona Wilderness Bill, which would have protected vast tracts of the public domain from the Forest Service's disastrous multiple-use doctrine. The university protested that it had other ideas for the mountains' future, and, by way of compromise, the committee filed the high peaks of the range away in a proposed wilderness study area. A delighted university administration turned to its blueprints and refined its plans to clear away three thousand acres of forest along the range's two highest points, Mount Graham and Emerald Peak, for an astronomical complex that would house eighteen giant telescopes, among them the nascent 11.3-meter Columbus. But then another complication kept the university from immediately razing the area.

Ecologists call the mountains of the basin and range provinces of the greater Southwest "mountain islands," for they stand in roughly the same relation to the surrounding desert as an island does to the sea—wet islands in a vast arid ocean. Isolated from like ecological zones, the mountains harbor animal and plant populations that in time differentiate themselves from their kin, so that the same species of birds will have different song dialects and a cougar, say, in the Black Mountains of New Mexico will bear slightly different markings from one in the White Mountains of Arizona, a scant hundred miles away. For wide-ranging animals like the mountain lion and the black bear, which travel among the ranges through the network of riparian corridors, these differences will be small; but for more sedentary populations, they will become more and more pronounced as time passes. Atop Mount Graham, one such population—one of eighteen unique species that the mountain sheltered—held the space scientists at bay.

This was *Tamiasciurus hudsonicus grahamensis*, a subspecies of the common red squirrel, a denizen of the spruce-fir forests of the mountain islands. Long a target of hunters who presumably prized the animal more for its coat than for the small meal it provides, the Mount Graham red squirrel population had declined by the early 1980s to only thirty or so mating pairs, no more than a hundred individuals in all, a count small enough to warrant its being entered on the federal roster of endangered species. Although in times of want the squirrel descends into the lower mixed-conifer zone, its preferred habitat is the highest peaks of the Pinaleños—exactly where the University of Arizona wanted to build its astronomical complex, in partnership with the Smithsonian Institution, the Vatican Observatory, the University of Chicago, and the Max Planck Institute of Germany.

Owing to the endangered status of *Tamiasciurus hudsonicus gra-hamensis*, the U.S. Fish and Wildlife Service ordered that the telescope complex not be built until it conducted a thoroughgoing environmental impact study, as mandated by the National Environmental Policy Act of 1970. Fearing that the Fish and Wildlife Service would eventually determine (as some of its officers were then arguing) that the red squirrel habitat be closed to any development whatever, and that the Pinaleños be readmitted into the Arizona Wilderness Bill, the University of Arizona went to war. Its administration hired the Washington law firm of Patton, Biggs and Blow, which had engineered the multibillion-dollar Chrysler Corporation bailout of the early 1980s, to lobby Arizona's congressional delegation and members of the House Interior Committee to hold Mount Graham exempt from a constellation of environmental protection laws and the provisions of the Endangered Species Act. (Arizona senator John McCain reportedly told director James Abbott that if these exemptions were not forthcoming he "would be the shortest-tenured supervisor in the history of the Forest Service.") Millions of dollars later the university had its way. Although Arizona voters overwhelmingly opposed the scopes, Morris Udall (the best representative Alaska ever had, people around here were once fond of saying) and his colleagues endorsed a rider to the Arizona-Idaho Conservation Bill of 1988 that left the high Pinaleños open to construction. Top University of Arizona administrators and astronomers celebrated this legislative end run by throwing a party, the centerpiece of which was a papier-mâché piñata in the shape of a Mount Graham red squirrel.

The lobbying worked both ways, however. Thanks to the efforts of the Sierra Club Legal Defense Fund and agitation from Earth First!, Greenpeace, the Audubon Society, and other environmental groups, Congress whittled the university's original demands down to an 8.6-acre site that would house eight telescopes. In the ensuing chain of injunctions and counterinjunctions, the Fish and Wildlife Service demanded that an environmental impact study be conducted despite the congressional ruling, and even the Forest Service agreed that the law must be obeyed. Environmental organizations nationwide joined the cause, and the University of Arizona administration building became the site of frequent demonstrations of the sort Tucson had not seen since the early 1970s. The leaders of the San Carlos Apache nation, whose domain included the Pinaleño Mountains until 1877, when Anglo miners began to strip them for their minerals and metals, reminded the university that mountaintops are properly sacred in Apache belief and suggested that enough summits had already been sacrificed for science. They also pointed out the impropriety of studying the cosmos with materials like steel and glass that had been violently wrested from the earth. Even the popular mystery writer Tony Hillerman weighed in, remarking that to build scopes atop Mount Graham "would be as bad as the Israeli government putting a radar tower on top of the Church of the Holy Sepulchre."

The presiding judges of the Ninth Federal Circuit Court ruled in favor of the protesters one day, the astronomical coalition the next, adding to the mounting tangle of legal claims on both sides. And so it went for the next two years, with construction delays costing the University of Arizona—or rather the taxpayers of Arizona—$25,000 a day, the equivalent of an assistant professor's annual salary.

The university eventually broke through. During a lull in the legal combat during the summer of 1990, the judges having momentarily rested in its favor, the university ordered its lumber crew to clearcut the Mount Graham site. In a few hours' time some two hundred and fifty old-growth spruce and fir fell before a battery of chain saws, and another three hundred saplings were removed and replanted down the slope. (Half have since died.) Red squirrel middens were bulldozed, a construction road was hurriedly scraped into the rocky forest floor, and the issue of Mount Graham descended from abstraction into bitter reality.

When the 1991 winter's accumulation of snow had melted, the remaining legal arguments against the scopes had been turned away from the bench. The university proceeded with the construction of the scopes, having lost several of its original partners, only to discover that its architects had miscalculated the prevailing wind patterns at the turbulent "tree layer," whereupon it petitioned the government to move the entire facility higher up the slope. And, as anticipated, the red squirrel population began to decline almost immediately, since its preferred habitat had been chewed up and spat out.

The astronomical complex atop Mount Graham can be of no possible benefit to any biotic community other than *Homo sapiens bureaucratensis,* whose comfortable lives are measured in federal grants. The administration's actions have made many new enemies for the University of Arizona, especially among those who are expected to pony up its operating budget year after year, and alienated thousands of alumni. And, ironically, the scopes will be of marginal value to the international community of astronomers and space scientists, for direct observation of the heavens yields little important data these days, as the recent Hubble Telescope debacle made clear. Instead, radio telescopy, which can be conducted from the plains of Kansas or the suburbs of Florida as profitably as it can from the top of a southern Arizona mountain, has become the mainstay of contemporary astronomical research. Mount Graham, it is now abundantly clear, was sacrificed not for knowledge but mere power.

The Mount Graham red squirrel, so seemingly insignificant, is but one of thousands of species and subspecies marched off to extinction in the twentieth century at the hands of humankind. It may be that *Tamiasciurus hudsonicus grahamensis* will find a new habitat in the mixed-conifer zone below the high peaks, but its survival is improbable in the extreme. No one can foresee the effects of its absence, but it will surely be felt on the mountain, for small creatures are invariably more important to a habitat than its megafauna; a honeybee shapes an environment far more profoundly than does an elk. The owls and hawks and eagles that feed on the red squirrel must find new prey or move on, the pine cones that sustained the Mount Graham red squirrel will go ungathered, and the *T. h. grahamensis* subspecies itself will perhaps be remembered only through a piñata and a few stuffed specimens gathered surreptitiously by University of Arizona biologists.

The heart of the issue is not the red squirrel, for its population had dwindled to the point where recovery may not have been possible in any event. Extinction is not the exception but the norm in life, and extinction may have been the squirrel's only future. The issue is the mountain itself. Mount Graham stands as a small example of the rapacity of modern corporatism, of which the modern university and scientific community are an integral part. A tract of 8.6 acres seems scarcely worth noticing in the face of corporatism's recent accomplishments: since 1970, after all, more than a million acres of old-growth forest have been clearcut in the United States alone, and today more than fifty-three acres of rain forest are felled globally every minute. The 8.6 acres of ancient forest atop the Pinaleño Mountains were clearcut by the colluding first-world powers of science, government, and academia, an unholy trinity that serves commerce to produce the earth's larger losses.

The tale of Mount Graham is an old, old story, repeated many times and in many places. In the third-century *Aesopica* you will find a fable that may well have been set alongside the banks of the Gila River at the dawn of the new millennium. It reads:

An astronomer used to wander outside each night to look at the stars. One evening, as he walked through town staring at the sky, he fell into a deep well. He cried for help until a neighbor arrived and called down to him. Learning what had happened, the neighbor said, "Why pry into the heavens when you can't see what's right here on Earth?"

But such blindness is pandemic in our time. Our rivers and mountains and forests are treated as commodities, our backcountry as a source of riches. One bureaucrat, the since-impeached Arizona governor Evan Mecham, even authorized a law allowing the state of Arizona to sell its riverbeds for $25 an acre to sand and gravel companies, extending a longstanding law that allowed private concerns to own nonnavigable streambeds. The steam shovels had just begun to bite into the bed of the Gila when a state appeals court struck Mecham's order down three years later on the proper grounds that it violated the state's responsibility to guard the public trust.

When the land is not seen as a place from which to extract wealth, it becomes a place in which to dump the trash. Manufacturing plants, airports, military installations, and sewage treatment plants have long disposed of hazardous wastes in the Gila and its tributaries. In 1987 the federal government planned to build a nuclear waste facility near Duncan, alongside the Gila, and only when the people of Greenlee County organized in opposition did the government withdraw the plan. (Downriver, west of Phoenix, stands the Palo Verde Generating Station, the largest nuclear power plant in the country. Its 670 million-gallon cooling pond uses water at the rate of 60,000 gallons a minute.) At the same time, the Bureau of Indian Affairs routinely dumped electrical transformers containing polychlorinated biphenyls (PCBs) alongside reservoirs and cattle tanks on the San Carlos Reservation, where the streamside soil had long been contaminated by previous diesel fuel dumping. It will cost taxpayers at least $4 million to remove these carcinogenic materials from the soil. In the meanwhile, Apaches are again dying at the hands of the American government.

The human population of the Southwest continues to grow and, with it, the number and kind of threats to those few ecosystems that remain intact. In 1990, Phoenix ranked as the ninth largest city in the United States, and by all projections its size will double within two generations. The Southwest is now the nation's fastest growing region, and the developers and boomers and acolytes of the short term work fervently to extract every ounce of potential from the already strained land. They no longer bother even to disguise their motives or sugar-coat their words; said one at a 1992 conference of so-called resource planners, "Something must be done to augment our water supplies so the Southwest can continue to drive our economy."

What that something may turn out to be, no one knows. The developers have bandied about any number of outlandish proposals, among them the construction of new canals tapping into the Columbia and the Mississippi, seeding the clouds to draw out the last of the rains, and floating icebergs from the Arctic by fast tugboats. No doubt Southwesterners will have to endure even stranger ideas in the years to come. This is a strange place, where the surrealism quotient out-paces that of every other American region. And in the Southwest, the more outlandish an idea is, the more likely it will find support.

All life is animated water.
—VLADIMIR VERNADSKY

9

REGAINING PARADISE

San Juan Day, June 24, and once again the rains have not yet come. As they have for centuries, the Tohono O'odham have made their saguaro wine, drunk it, and called up the rain clouds, but the rain clouds have yet to materialize. Only a few years ago an elderly Tohono O'odham man confessed to ethnobiologist Gary Paul Nabhan, "I still believe in Jesus and the saints, but I know too that when we drink the wine and sing I'itoi's help, the rains always come." But I'itoi, Elder Brother, the creator god of this dry stretch of universe, seems to have overslept this year, fast in his cave in the heart of Baboquívari Mountain.

Summer has come to the desert, a season punctuated only by small changes in the intense heat of day, when the dawn brings a wall of glaring white light upon the land, washing out its colors, when human and animal life slows to torpor until night has fallen. Those foolish enough to stay willingly in the desert in summertime—the mark, folks say around here, of the true desert rat—eat bushels of fruit, seek shade and breezes, and keep abundant liquids within easy reach, knowing only that the next few months will bring the same heat, day after day, hour after hour. You dare not read Raymond Chandler's short story "Red Wind" for fear that this time, yes, the heat will prove too much for the murderer within.

But the season usually brings rain as well, often half the rain that will fall each year on the Sonoran Desert. The lightning-lashed rise of an afternoon storm in this season is enough to give birth to a new theology, as deserts have bred the world's great faiths. It is a fine and oppressive time. It makes one think of water, of the open sea, of ice-cold beer.

As I have been writing this book I have been thinking of rivers. I have been thinking of the rivers I have seen: the Thames, the Potomac, the Danube, the Mississippi, the Tiber, the Lerma, the Rhine, the Black Warrior, the Seine. Even the Hudson. (Has there ever been a tribe to bestow an ugly name upon a river? Their appellations sing. Even Dry Beaver Creek, in central Arizona, has its charm.) And I have been thinking of rivers I have never seen but hope to stand alongside one day: the Lena, the Brahmaputra, the Blue Nile, the Mackenzie, the Volga, the Amazon, the Ganges, the Yangtze. And the Gila and its many tributaries.

For the most part we know the rivers of the desert only by their absence, only as tiny blue scratches, separated by ellipses, on highway maps, in the cartographic code for the dead. The desiccated beds of those once great rivers, spanned by unsteady bridges, mock their intended function, carrying runoff from the heavens only a few days of the year, effluent from sewage treatment plants with greater regularity. For the rest of the year, bone-dry, they serve as dragstrips for three-wheeled recreational vehicles, as dumping grounds for unwanted mattresses and house pets, for defaulting cocaine consumers. They are rivers in name only, an insult to the theory and practice of flowing water.

To bring back the old rivers is not an impossibility; to declare that time cannot be reversed is mere dogma. But to regain the Gila, the Colorado, the San Pedro—residents of any other town west of the hundredth meridian need only substitute appropriate names for the rivers they have lost—will require an absolute change in the politics and economics of the American West, away from the ceaseless rapacity that has characterized the last century and toward a more sustainable ethic, one that recognizes water as the best of all clean industries, the best, as Herakleitos says, of all things.

Neither is to bring back the rivers mere wishful thinking. Rivers run as they will, despite the tethers we place on them; so long as water flows on earth, it will somehow find its way to the sea. In 1992 and 1993, water flowed through the desert in abundance, thanks to the influence of the El Niño weather pattern, which rises in the western Pacific and directs winter storms northeastward to the Hawaiian Islands and thence to the coasts of California and Mexico.

The winter of 1992 brought El Niño storms crashing into the tall mountains where the Gila is born, swiftly filling the rivulets and creeks and main channels with cold surging water. During two months of rain I followed the river from its source to its confluence with the Colorado, watching with amazement and pleasure as the river flowed over manmade restraints and roared through its normally dry bed, past the vast orange groves and palm stands of then-inundated western Arizona. The winter of 1993 brought still more rain, causing $200 million in damage along the Gila's length. There were times in January when I could swear I saw the neighborhood animals lining up two by two.

The floods came as no surprise to longtime Southwesterners. The desert, they know, has its cycles: some years it rains, some years it

A freeflowing river above the Gila Box, near Safford, Arizona.
(Photograph by the author)

doesn't. El Niño brought plentiful rain to mark the onset of the 1990s, with wet winters and comparatively dry summers, the supposed "monsoon season." For the second time in a decade, most of New Mexico's and Arizona's rivers surged to so-called hundred-year flood levels, which, as the name implies, should occur but once in a century. The Verde River, a major tributary of the middle Gila, did even better, cresting to the thousand-year mark.

The floods had their surprises nonetheless. The developers who chose to build apartment complexes and shopping centers on obvious floodplains wondered why their properties had gone sailing off to Mexico. The residents of Winkelman Flats seemed to be taken aback by the raging Gila, which made off with their horse trailers and toolsheds and homes. Yuma farmers were stunned by their waterlogged fields and damaged crops. And the engineers who continue to channelize and dam Arizona's streams and rivers, hoping to tame them, wondered why nature refused to submit to their will.

Dams, as has been proved in many places at many times, cannot permanently thwart nature. When the great rains of October 1983 came, the rusty floodgates at Coolidge Dam failed to open. Glen Canyon Dam, on the Colorado, shivered loose from its bedding in soft sandstone, and its operators sounded a warning that it might collapse at any minute—taking with it, in turn, Hoover Dam, Davis Dam, Parker Dam, and Imperial Dam. By some miracle it stood, but dozens of earthen check dams crumbled across the Southwest.

January 1993 brought worse news for the dam builders. By the 11th the Gila was flowing at 30,000 cubic feet per second, twenty times its normal load; Coolidge Dam again failed to do its putative job, and it released a dozen times more water than it did in 1983. Throughout the Southwest buckled roadways and shorn bridges, inundated fields and waterlogged crops, dismantled apartments and mangled automobiles, silt-covered floors and shattered lives attested to weeks of rain.

The sight of so much flowing water, of a Gila running fast and, for all purposes, free, gave much hope as well to those who seek to put it in that condition permanently. The Gila watershed may have witnessed many extinctions, many instances of environmental and social degradation, but it also has given rise to a number of protectors, among them modern activists Dave Foreman, from the little headwaters town of Reserve, and M. H. Salmon, now of Silver City; both have been important advocates against damming and for wilderness. They have as their distinguished predecessor one of the greatest American conservationists of them all, who formulated his ideas on preservation and sustainable use while working as a forest ranger in the Black Mountains.

He was Aldo Leopold, and he began his service in 1909 as an obedient soldier in Gifford Pinchot's multiple-use army. Stationed in various public-domain forests of Arizona and New Mexico, far from his native Iowa and farther still from the textbooks that had first shaped his ideas on forestry, Leopold still acted as most rangers of the time did—as a hired gun for the railroads and ranchers. But in time the wild mountains and rivers exercised their magic on him, and Leopold underwent a transformation that in time would put him squarely at odds with an array of interests, not the least of them the bureaucracy he had until then faithfully served.

The critical moment came, Leopold wrote in his now-classic *Sand County Almanac*, when he killed an old wolf in a valley along the San Francisco River. He and his companions fired round after round into the wolf and her pups, then scrambled down the embankment from which they had been shooting to tally up the score. As he recalled,

We reached the old wolf in time to watch a fierce green fire dying in her eyes. . . . I was young then, and full of trigger-itch; I

thought that because fewer wolves meant more deer, no wolves would mean hunters' paradise. But after seeing the green fire die, I sensed that neither the wolf nor the mountain agreed with such a view. . . . The cowman who cleans his range of wolves does not realize that he is taking over the wolf's job of trimming the herd to fit the range. He has not learned to think like a mountain. Hence we have dustbowls, and rivers washing the future into the sea.

His apostasy complete, Leopold went on to urge that cattle be kept off the public lands as much as was possible—he later tempered his temperance and suggested the number be none—and that the Forest Service turn its attention less to serving the interests of a few ranchers and more to protecting the public domain for the good of the future. This was no mere rhetoric; when Leopold managed the Tonto National Forest he ordered an immediate reduction of cattle, some 50,000 head of which had been browsing the forest undergrowth to stubble. But then America entered the First World War, demand increased for "bully beef" to feed the troops, and Leopold's order was rescinded; a local rancher later recalled, "We reduced all the way up to 82,000 head!"

After the war Leopold was promoted to assistant district forester over the twenty million acres of Forest Service holdings in the Southwest, and he spent more and more time in the field, especially at the headwaters of the Gila. He described it as it was then: an area "topographically isolated by mountain ranges and box canyons. It has not yet been penetrated by railroads and only to a very limited extent by roads. . . . It is the last typical wilderness in the southwestern mountains." Leopold set to work campaigning for the creation of the first nationally designated wilderness area, and to his surprise his proposal was approved. On June 3, 1924, Congress set aside nearly 755,000

The high beginnings of the Gila Wilderness above Cliff, New Mexico.
(Photograph by the author)

acres of land in the Gila River Forest Reserve. Today the Gila Wilderness and the adjoining Aldo Leopold Wilderness make up nearly a million acres of protected land within the still-overlogged, three-million-acre Gila National Forest.

The following year Leopold issued a pamphlet called "The Watershed Handbook" to his colleagues. Restating some of John Wesley Powell's arguments on the watershed as an ecological and—potentially—political unit, it met with a still-hostile audience among his fellow forest rangers. In it can be found the seeds of what Leopold would call the "land ethic," an elegantly simple declaration of rights for soil, water, wind, plants, and animals: "A thing is right when it tends to preserve the integrity, stability, and beauty of the biotic community. It is wrong when it tends otherwise."

The Forest Service, Leopold concluded, was an agent of otherwise-tending change in the lands it was assigned to preserve. He did not shy from pointing out his own role in the mass slaughter of large predators in the Southwestern forests:

> *We forest officers, who acquiesced in the extinguishment of the bear, knew a local rancher who had plowed up a dagger engraved with the name of one of Coronado's captains. We spoke harshly of the Spanish who, in their zeal for gold and converts, had needlessly extinguished the native Indians. It did not occur to us that we, too, were the captains of an invasion too sure of its own righteousness.*

Such openness would not make him many friends in the developing states of Arizona and New Mexico, and in any event Leopold was not long for the Southwest. In 1924 he was transferred to Madison, Wisconsin, and assigned to the U.S. Forest Products Laboratory, where Forest Service scientists thought up inventive new uses for the trees they ostensibly protected. He remained with the Forest Service for a few more years, then helped found both the Wilderness Society and the Civilian Conservation Corps. For the remainder of his life he worked on preservation issues and wrote hundreds of elegant essays. He died on April 21, 1948, of a heart attack while helping a Wisconsin neighbor fight a small grass fire. Leopold's lifework, however, endures, and few American naturalists and conservation workers have not been influenced by his writings.

Among Leopold's contributions was the idea that wilderness areas be made as large as possible, if for no other reason than to enable what Thoreau called "the preservation of the world." In this he was, as usual, prescient, for later generations of scientists and ecologists have determined that animal species need ample room if their gene pools are to remain open-ended and therefore healthy, and they have recognized as well that large territories allow for isolation, the sine qua non for speciation. In recent years the distinguished biologist E. O. Wilson has noted that the number of species doubles with every ten-fold increase in untrammeled area, and other studies have borne out his projections.

Consider, for example, the spotted owl, each individual of which requires three to eight square kilometers of coniferous forest at least 250 years old in order to flourish. The Southwestern spotted owl population has declined exactly in proportion with the loss of this habitat; its cousin in the Pacific Northwest will almost certainly decline altogether as the old-growth forests tumble before loggers' chain saws. Great raptors like the eagle require even more land, some twenty-five square miles of relatively pristine terrain over which to hold dominion, if they are to scare up sufficient game to survive.

Even in large tracts of roadless wilderness, like the 1.5-million-acre Gila/Black preserve, there is not sufficient space for the full speciation on which natural ecosystems depend. The sole solution is to add new tracts of land to existing wilderness areas and to set aside whole new areas, such as the Utah Wilderness Coalition's recent proposal to create a five-million-acre preserve embracing most of the southern part of that state, including the "Golden Circle" of Arches, Canyonlands, Bryce Canyon, Capitol Reef, and Zion national parks. This would be an important development, for most of our national parks and forests and wildlife refuges—decried since their founding as "reservoirs of predation"—are little improvement over zoos in protecting animals because of their inadequate habitat size.

Wilson has remarked that "wilderness has virtue unto itself and needs no extraneous justification" and that, if it does, we can find in its preservation enough enlightened self-interest, in the form of, say, the potential of a new pharmacopoeia derived from plants that are not yet known or well studied; "the wildlands," as he says, "are like a magic well: the more that is drawn from them in knowledge and benefits, the more there will be to draw." (Saint Bernard of Clairvaux noted another benefit: "You will find something more in woods than in books," he said. "Trees and stones will teach you that which you can never learn from masters.") Regrettably, Wilson's view is far from universal, and there are still too many scientists at the public trough who busy themselves rummaging through the genetic toolbox to invent giant chickens and eugenically satisfactory humans. They would do better, clearly, to join Wilson in figuring out how to preserve what little of the world we still have, or it, too, will be gone. As Douglas Chadwick has remarked in summarizing Wilson's chief contribution to scientific theory, "The main lesson of island biogeography is this: we cannot tuck species away in little preserves as if we were storing pieces in a museum, then come back a century later and expect to find them still there."

Taking the lead from the Utah Wilderness Coalition, Southwestern activists need not be modest. Dave Foreman's recent call for the establishment of multimillion-acre wilderness areas throughout Arizona and New Mexico, for instance, pales with the proposal Rutgers University geographers Frank Popper and Deborah Popper have advanced for the Great Plains. They have noted that the Ogallala Aquifer, which underlies 1,375,000 square miles of high prairie, is being overdrafted fifty times faster than it can be replenished, a rate steeper by five times than the worst current overdrafting in the Southwest. The twenty million acre feet of water annually pumped from the Ogallala Aquifer nourish 20 percent of the irrigated farmland in America, and those farms are sure to fail as this ancient source of water dries up. (The 1988 drought on the plains cut our national grain production by 40 percent.) In the early 1980s the farm and livestock lobbies petitioned President Ronald Reagan to authorize funds to build an irrigation canal from the Great Lakes—which contain the world's largest supply of freshwater—across the Great Plains, from Minnesota to

Texas. Reagan's aides, noting the failure of irrigation projects in the West to pay for themselves, demanded proof that 35 percent of the construction costs could be guaranteed within twenty years, and when the lobbyists answered that such proof could not be mustered, the project died. For their part, the Poppers call for a turn in the opposite direction. They argue that as the plains are necessarily abandoned, native ecosystems be allowed to return, replacing introduced grains with indigenous tallgrasses. In the light of their proposal—which has many merits, among them its recognition of "natural nations" based on watersheds—the notion of adding on a couple of million acres to the present Gila Wilderness seems modest indeed.

There is still more to be done. One of the first needs is to set about reforesting the Gila highlands. Our model can be the Civilian Conservation Corps' (CCC) work in the West in the 1930s and 1940s—thanks again in some measure to the benevolent hand of Aldo Leopold—when millions upon millions of trees were planted. (On average the CCC spent $85.50 per capita in the Western states, as against $19.50 nationwide, so bad was the problem of clearcutting.) The corps employed some fifteen thousand Indians to restore reservation tracts, including great parcels on the San Carlos and White Mountain Apache nations, and in its first year of operation alone the CCC had improved millions of acres of public land.

Without reforestation, the tremendous erosion that has been taking place along the Gila watershed for a century and a half can only grow worse in the coming years. Frank H. Olmstead warned nine decades ago, "It is up to the men of this generation to meet the situation manfully and to utilize fully every resource at the command of the Nation . . . if we are not to lose what we have so carelessly guarded from the date of our possession in 1848 to this time." He was not heeded, nor have his likeminded peers been heeded then or since. Across the nation we are losing the most precious natural re-

The loss of topsoil means an end to farming of inappropriate crops.
This farmworker's abandoned mobile home near Hyder, Arizona,
bespeaks a change of fortunes. (Photograph by the author)

source: its topsoil. Now, only 11 percent of the surface of the earth is
arable; a great portion of that productive land lies within the United
States. But thanks to industrial agriculture, with its destructive demand
for overproduction, its refusal to allow land to lie fallow, to plow along
contours, to treat the soil as a living entity, and thanks to industrial
logging in the highlands, some 35 percent of the nation's topsoil—
formed in geological time, the result of weathering and the decay of
dead plants and animals, essentially nonrenewable—has been lost,
washed, or blown away. In the twisted language of the agroindustri-
alists, it has for a century been more "cost-effective" to allow that loss
rather than conserve the soil, the occasional dust bowl be damned. In
the last two decades more than four million acres of productive crop-

land annually have been lost forever through erosion; every bushel of Iowa corn costs two bushels of topsoil to produce, every calorie of food costs ten calories of energy, an intolerably misguided economy of waste.

We need to found a modern analog to the CCC if our mountains are not to suffer further damage. As the most casual observation will indicate, mere gravity pulls down everything that can be pulled—rocks, trees, water. Only a healthy cover of plants can hold mountain soil in place, and only a concerted effort or the magical disappearance of humans and cattle will ever put that cover in place.

In reforesting we must also reeducate the U.S. Forest Service. Gifford Pinchot's notion of the service as a body of economic advisors who counsel industry on the use of trees needs to be discarded, the doctrine of multiple use abandoned. That reeducation had better come fast, for the agency is blind to the lessons of preservation, to the fact that it directly subsidizes a marginal industry. Even as I write, the Forest Service is hurrying to build 43,000 miles of new roads—adding to the 360,000 already in our national forests—so that new areas cannot be designated as wilderness and thus removed from the sawyers' blades.

It should be noted, although the lumber industry would not want it widely known, that sustainable forestry is possible. Loggers can, if they choose, remove some mature trees from a forest and not clear the underbrush in doing so, and the forest would very easily recover. Leaving a few felled logs behind would further generate additional mycorrhizae that allow other plants to grow. In forests where this method has been tried new growth occurs far more quickly than in clearcut areas, and both the presence of undergrowth and the habit of random logging help to maintain the genetic diversity that is so often lacking in our national forests, which resemble nothing so much as tree farms. That diversity is critical. As ecologist Ramón Mergalef has remarked, late stages of succession in climax or old-growth forests are stable precisely because of their diversity; they are resistant to diseases and ecological invaders, and they restrain great increases in natural populations of all kinds. Henry David Thoreau put it another way: "In a wood that has been left alone for the longest period the greatest regularity and harmony in the disposition of the trees will be observed, while in our ordinary woods man has often interfered and favored the growth of other kinds than are best fitted to grow there naturally."

The work of a few hands in a forest can yield wonders. In Auroville, India, near Pondicherry, an international religious community has planted over a million trees in the last twenty years on two thousand acres of dry plateau. Formerly barren and bereft of life, the plateau now teems with species that had abandoned the plateau when the old-growth forest was cleared for fuel, and the project has been so successful that the Indian government has commissioned Auroville to undertake tree-planting campaigns elsewhere in the country. Similarly, let us recall Jean Giono's famed account of shepherd Elzéard Bouffier's single-handed campaign in the Provençe, *The Man Who Planted Trees*. By the end of the nineteenth century charcoal makers had deforested the land; the streams had died, and southern Provençe looked much like the Sahel. Beginning in 1914, Bouffier planted hundreds of thousands of trees on the denuded hillsides, and a vast deciduous forest now stands to commemorate his work.

Another step in reclaiming the Gila watershed is to reeducate the Bureau of Land Management (BLM), whose critics have properly renamed it the Bureau of Livestock and Mining. The first step is to remove most cattle from the public lands of the West, recognizing that in the end the land can simply not sustain this eminently marginal economic activity. When cattle are removed a place often recovers remarkably swiftly. The Blue River tributary of the Gila, for instance, was so overgrazed by the 1920s that its basal soils had washed out, leaving only a succession of ghost towns and abandoned peach orchards to attest that humans had once been there. Cattle were removed from the lower Blue in the middle 1980s, and at the same time a great swath of tamarisk trees were uprooted. Only a few years later the cottonwood-willow-sycamore associations are beginning to return to the once-ravaged landscape, and there is every reason to believe that similar recoveries will be the norm on other parts of the river.

"The deserts should never be reclaimed," wrote the acclaimed desert rat John Van Dyke at the turn of the century. "They are the breathing-spaces of the west and should be preserved forever." For too long the BLM has been in the business precisely of reclaiming the lands under its jurisdiction for the benefit of the few. The agency manages 85,000 miles of streams and rivers and 164 million acres of public grazing lands, and the sorry state of land and water alike in this country is testimony to its corruption.

If we are to undertake Frank Olmstead's challenge to combat erosion, we will need to set an agricultural revolution in motion—on the Gila, and throughout America. Wendell Berry has observed in *The Unsettling of America* and elsewhere that as our agriculture becomes ever more industrialized, its destructive manifestations become more and more pronounced. One of them is the rise of monoculture, the production of but a few "scientifically" selected varieties of food crops and the loss of genetic diversity that has come with it. As a result of the demands of industrialized, standardized agriculture, for example, of the seven thousand varieties of apples that have been developed in the United States, only four are generally available today: the Delicious, McIntosh, Winesap, and Jonathan, a meager table indeed. (The journalist and food critic A. J. Liebling wrote half a century ago, "People who don't like food have made a triumph of the Delicious because it doesn't taste like an apple, and of the Golden Delicious because it doesn't taste like anything.") As with such machine-produced items

as metal bolts and pencils, the rise of industrialization in food production has led directly to an impoverishment of forms, a loss of the
necessary complexity that informs any art rightly practiced and a dim-
inution of choice.

But appropriate agriculture, like appropriate forestry and appropriate ranching, is possible. In the arid Southwest, appropriate agriculture naturally means farming crops that do not require much water.
While only a few dozen species of plants are fully utilized in the modern diet of industrialized societies—the most important being wheat,
rice, maize, and potatoes—the Sonoran Desert alone boasts more than
2,500 native species of food plants. In a regime of appropriate agriculture many more of them can be utilized effectively both to increase
the local menu of foodstuffs and to battle monoculture.

Some Gila-watershed farmers are already producing arid-land
crops. On the lower Gila now lie vast fields of jojoba (*Simmondsia
chinensis*), a bushy plant whose bean yields an oil that is nearly identical
in chemical composition to spermaceti, the oil produced by sperm
whales. This imperishable oil is extremely versatile: it can be used for
cooking, in shampoos and soaps and cars, in medicines and industrial
lubricants. (In the last use another Gila native, lesquerella [*Lesquerella
fendleri*], shows promise as well.) Jojoba may become a major cash
crop in the Southwest, especially as the industrialized world continues
to deplete the planet's supply of fossil fuels.

In his recent book *The Diversity of Life*, E. O. Wilson reports that
a Mexican graduate student recently located in the state of Jalisco a
small field of *Zea diploperennis*, a wild relative of corn that was once
thought to be extinct. (This patch was doomed to be cleared, and had
the student not been a gifted persuader it may well not have survived
the season.) *Zea diploperennis* may be introduced into various strains
of *Zea mays*, our common food corn, and with it production will surely
rise; a hybrid would be both disease- and drought-resistant and, unlike

most domesticated corn, would grow perennially. This, too, promises a new, appropriate crop for the Gila watershed.

Other native plants can readily supplant marginal exotic plants as cash crops. Buffalo gourd (*Cucurbita foetidissima*), for instance, produces edible oil and grows on land unsuitable for most agriculture; halophytes such as saltbush (*Atriplex*) and Palmer's saltgrass (*Distichlis palmeri*), which grow in salty and even oceanic water, can replace alfalfa as fodder—and yield twice as much produce an acre. And thanks to growing cosmopolitanism in culinary matters in this and other countries, crops like chiltepin (*Capsicum annuum aviculare*), a pepper that ethnobotanist Gary Paul Nabhan calls "the red-hot mother of all chiles," are in wide demand, only second in cash value to saffron.

Even introduced plants have prospects. One is the neem tree (*Azadirochta indica*), a native of India, drought-tolerant and apparently compatible with native American desert vegetation. One of its wonders is that it produces natural pesticides that can easily replace chemical ones, thus allowing for the continued health of Mexican free-tail bats and agaves, of white-winged sphinx moths and saguaro cacti. The neem tree has been called "the village pharmacy," too, for the medicines its bark yields, and Indians who use its twigs as toothbrushes reportedly suffer far fewer dental problems than does the general population of the subcontinent. Other wonders await us in arid lands elsewhere on the planet, and they need not be horrors like tamarisk, cheatgrass, and tumbleweed.

"Should trees have standing?" asked Christopher Stone, a legal scholar, in his book of that name. Answering affirmatively, Stone argued that nature be allowed its day in court and protected by law from further encroachment. Echoing Stone, we might ask, should rivers have rights?

Yes, they should.

In our time, while the Amazon is burning and America's grain belt is withering away and the Aral Sea is disappearing, our courts have ruled that keeping water in rivers for the health of fish populations is not beneficial use, but that overallocating it for farming is. In our time—in late August of 1992, to be precise—the Bureau of Land Management attempted to designate fourteen miles of the upper Gila River near Safford as a roadway, both so that drivers of off-road vehicles could tear around in the riverbed with impunity and so that the river and its nearby tributaries could be exempted from consideration as wild and scenic rivers under the recent congressional act of that name. Given such actions, we can do far worse than press for the rights of our waterways immediately.

There are reasons to be hopeful. One is the passage, after years of legislative debate, of the national Omnibus Water Act of 1992. Among other things, the act requires that Western cities reserve large amounts of water to repair the environmental damage their sources of water have sustained: 800,000 acre feet of the water previously allocated to farmers in central California, for example, now annually must go to recharge the rivers and streams of the Sacramento and San Joaquin valleys.

The work of the national Nature Conservancy offers hope as well. The private group has recently acquired a sixty-nine-acre tract of palustrine wetlands at the confluence of San Pedro and Gila rivers called Cooks Lake, one of Arizona's few wooded swamps, and it plans to convert several hundred additional acres of adjoining land to mesquite bosques. (The area had supposedly been "protected" by the provisions of the Clean Water Act, but instead was full of mine tailings from the nearby ASARCO smelter.) The San Pedro is one of only four American rivers to harbor significant quantities of mesquite, and along its course lie extremely valuable wildlife refuges that shelter fifty-five species of endangered animals, among them the peregrine falcon (*Falco peregrinus*); the gray hawk (*Buteo nitidus*), of which only fifty-four nesting pairs are thought to exist in the United States; the yellow-billed cuckoo (*Coccyzus americanus*); the vermilion flycatcher (*Pyrocephalus rubinus*); Costa's hummingbird (*Archilochus costae*); Bell's vireo (*Vireo bellii*); and the last ocelots (*Felis pardalis*), a globally endangered cat, known to exist in the lowlands of the Gila watershed.

The preservation of the San Pedro, which the Nature Conservancy has deemed one of the world's "last great places," is especially important given the overall decline in riparian habitats and consequently in migratory bird populations throughout the Western Hemisphere. The black-crowned night-heron (*Nycticorax nycticorax*), for instance, once lived in huge colonies along watercourses throughout the Southwest, including the Gila and its tributaries. When these disappeared so did the bird, and a decade ago the species was threatened with extirpation. The restoration of rivers like the San Pedro, coupled with the recent increased rains through the El Niño weather system, has brought the bird back to the region; while the population is not yet thriving, it at least shows the promise of reestablishing itself over time. We can resuscitate other ghosts, ghosts the poet Vachel Lindsay once conjured up:

> *When Daniel Boone goes by, at night,*
> *The phantom deer arise,*
> *And all lost, wild America,*
> *Is burning in their eyes.*

The restoration of the San Pedro provides a key for ways in which other Southwestern rivers can be brought back to life. River otters now swim freely in the lower Verde tributary of the Gila, thanks to individual initiative within the Arizona Game and Fish Department. In Florida, the Bureau of Reclamation is now "unreclaiming" the Kissimmee River, destroying old canals that in their turn destroyed wildlife habitats, just as projected dams along the Verde would have obliterated the last nesting habitats of the bald eagle in the Southwest. There is no reason the bureau could not direct its efforts to "unchannelizing" the Gila, the Salt, the Colorado.

All this is work for individuals and government alike. A farmer from Eloy, Arizona, not long ago donated a hundred miles of PVC irrigation pipe to a restoration initiative after the Central Arizona Project began to deliver water to her fields. The pipe was in turn used to irrigate a nascent cottonwood-willow-mesquite forest along fifteen miles of the Gila southwest of Buckeye, Arizona, on the middle Gila. Within our lifetime this may become a new analog to the famous New York Thicket that brought so much joy to the Akimel O'odham; may many more such places soon arise.

Finally, the dams that dot the rivers of the Southwest must be removed, one by one. To dam a river is only to pretend that risk can be minimized, and ours has been a risk-fearing age, to the great delight of insurance companies and cowards. Between 1962 and 1968 more than twelve hundred major dams were built throughout the United States, more than in any other single period in our history, and sixty thousand dams now dot the national landscape. Six hundred thousand miles of American rivers have been inundated by reservoirs, and millions of acres of land have been lost. But there is no way, in truth, to remove risk entirely from our lives, and to pretend otherwise is mere naivete. Wind eddies grow to be cyclones; rivulets swell to floods; and rivers, if they are rivers at all, will on occasion leave their banks for a sojourn on nearby floodplains. The time has come to dismantle the dams that choke the rivers of these arid lands. Southwesterners will have to make do without a few things in the process: the green lawns brought from points east as tokens of cooler Anglo-Saxon climes; golf courses that consume a million gallons of water a day; inexpensive winter vegetables and cheap abundant beef. It has been remarked that the earth can sustain billions of humans, but not 250 million Americans. In the Southwest, we can at least begin to effect changes that will make us better planetary citizens.

Wilderness is its own argument, E. O. Wilson has reminded us. So, too, are mountains. If self-interest must enter into our bargaining with nature, consider the role of mountains as a source of reverie. The great religions were born in the deserts of the world, but mountains provided their inspiration; as the psychologist Bernard S. Aaronson has observed, "The traditional association of mountain tops with the abode of Deity may be less because they are higher than the areas around them than because they make possible those experiences of expanded depth in which the self can invest itself in the world around it and expand across the valleys." Mountains have utilitarian value as well, as John Muir pointed out more than a century ago. "Thousands of tired, nerve-shaken, over-civilized people are beginning to find out that going to the mountains is going home."

So, too, are rivers their own argument. The lapping sound of their waters is the most primeval sound in the world, our Ur-song; small wonder that in India the insane are often tied to trees alongside a riverbank, where the water's music helps soothe the confusion within. Just as other cultures, as Claude Lévi-Strauss has reminded us, provide a tuning fork against which to sound our own, so the health of other species, the health of our woods and mountains and rivers, affords us a gauge by which to measure our own well-being. By this measure we are not doing so well, but in our recognizing this lies the germ of recovery.

The delicately balanced chain of life and the habitats of these arid places require constant protection, since humans, the chief agents of environmental change, are unlikely to alter their quotidian habits such that nature can put itself back in order. Where humans are not often found as permanent residents—the high country abutting the Gila's headwaters, for instance—there is perhaps less work to do, but everywhere the intramontane West offers ample opportunities to reduce the effects of industrial-age humans on natural populations. As Aldo Leopold observed, "We abuse land because we regard it as a commodity belonging to us. When we see land as a community to which we belong, we may begin to use it with love and respect." We can start by coming to know some of the animals that make their homes here, by paying closer attention to the lay of the land and the ineluctable rhythms of nature, by assuming guardianship of the rivers and mountains on which our lives ultimately depend. We can start by tending to our own garden, which is the world.

The nature of human beings is to dream. The nature of writers is to spin tales. It is time that we turn to better stories and dreams than the ones we have now.

A flowing Gila would be a start.

God made a song when the world was new,
Water, water, sings it through.
—ANGLO-SAXON LYRIC

BIBLIOGRAPHIC
ESSAY

For all its importance to the natural and human history of the greater Southwest, the Gila has inspired relatively few books. Two of the best known are Edwin Corle's *The Gila: River of the Southwest* (New York: Holt, Rinehart and Winston, 1951; reprint, Lincoln: University of Nebraska Press, 1963) and Ross Calvin's *River of the Sun* (Albuquerque: University of New Mexico Press, 1949). Corle's book is useful but dated, written at a time when the notion of conquering the wilderness was still a tenable doctrine in the eyes of most readers. Calvin's, the product of a minister, abounds with rhetorical flourishes and purple passages, but the affection he felt for the Gila and its tributaries comes through on each page.

M. H. Salmon's *Gila Descending* (Silver City, N.M.: High-Lonesome Books) is a delightful account of a canoe trip the author made down the upper Gila in the mid-1980s. A native of the headwaters, Salmon offers many sharp observations on the uses and misuses the upper river has been put to.

On the rivers of the Southwest, and on rivers generally, I have had the benefit of many useful books. Foremost among them are Edmund Andrews et al., *Colorado River Ecology and Dam Management* (Washington: National Academy Press, 1991); the Arizona Rivers Coalition, *Arizona Rivers: Lifeblood of the Desert* (Phoenix: ARC, 1991); Richard L. Berkman and W. Kip Viscusi's *Damming the West* (New York: Grossman, 1973); Charles Bowden's *Killing the Hidden Waters* (Austin: University of Texas Press, 1977); Philip L. Fradkin's *A River No More: The Colorado River and the West* (New York: Alfred A. Knopf, 1981); Paul Horgan's *Great River: The Rio Grande in North American History* (New York: Rinehart and Company, 1954); H. B. N. Hynes's *The Ecology of Running Waters* (Toronto: University of Toronto Press, 1970); Rich Johnson's *The Central Arizona Project, 1918–1968* (Tucson: University of Arizona Press, 1977); Ed Marston's edited volume *Western Water Made Simple* (Covelo, Calif.: Island Press, 1987); Frank H. Olmstead's *Gila River Flood Control* (Washington: Senate Document No. 436, 65th Congress, 3rd Session. Government Printing Office, 1919); Tim Palmer's *Endangered Rivers and the Conservation Movement* (Berkeley and Los Angeles: University of California Press, 1986); John Wesley Powell's *Lands of the Arid Region of the United States* (Washington: Government Printing Office, 1879); Marc Reisner's *Cadillac Desert: The American West and Its Disappearing Water* (New York: Viking Press, 1986); the Salt River Project's *The Taming of the Salt* (Phoenix: SRP, 1979); Bill Thomas's *American Rivers* (New York: W.W. Norton, 1978); John Walton's *Western Times and Water Wars* (Berkeley and Los Angeles: University of California Press, 1992); Frank Welsh's *How to Create a Water Crisis* (Boulder, Colo.: Johnson Books, 1985); and Donald Worster's *Rivers of Empire* (New York: Pantheon Books, 1985).

On the geology of the Gila watershed, I have consulted Chronic Halka's invaluable books *Roadside Geology of Arizona* (1983) and *Roadside Geology of New Mexico* (1987), both published by Mountain

Press Publishing of Missoula, Montana. John A. Jerome's lively book *On Mountains* (New York: Harcourt Brace Jovanovich, 1978) is a thorough look at geology from a lay point of view, focusing on the landforms of New England. John McPhee's *Basin and Range* (New York: Farrar, Straus and Giroux, 1980) is more exacting—McPhee is a master of encyclopedic detail—but equally pleasurable to read, as are the three other volumes in his Annals of the Former World series of books on American geomorphology. Dale Nations and Edward Stump's *Geology of Arizona* (Dubuque, Iowa: Kendall/Hunt Publishing Company, 1981) and Allan A. Schoenherr's *Natural History of California* (Berkeley and Los Angeles: University of California Press, 1992) offer a good overview of the geology of the Southwest as a whole. (I owe thanks here to Doug Shakel for his courses in geology at the University of Arizona.) Clyde P. Ross's *The Lower Gila Region, Arizona* (Washington: U.S. Geological Survey Water-Supply Paper 498. Government Printing Office, 1923) is a surprisingly engaging look at the tangled geomorphology of the western course of the river, and Joseph Wheeler's *Topographical and Geological Surveys* (Washington: U.S. Government Printing Office, 1873) contains a number of useful observations as well.

If you want to provoke an endless argument, set forth a hypothesis—any hypothesis—about the prehistory of North America. Specialists in the Southwest, who are legion, have yet to concur on cultural sequences or chronology, and the overall prehistory of the region undergoes substantial revision at least once a decade. The longtime dean of Southwestern archaeology, Emil W. Haury, was one of the first scholars to present large-scale studies of the area in books like *The Hohokam: Desert Farmers and Craftsmen* (1976) and *Prehistory of the American Southwest* (1986), while he wrote a number of useful smaller studies like *The Archaeology and Straitigraphy of Ventana Cave, Ari-*

zona (1966), all published by the University of Arizona Press. All of those books are now generally acknowledged to be well out of date, and they should be supplemented with Suzanne K. Fish et al., eds., *The Marana Community in the Hohokam World* (Tucson: Anthropological Papers of the University of Arizona Number 56, 1993), an important re-evaluation of Hohokam prehistory. Among more recent general studies the best and most accessible is Linda S. Cordell's *Prehistory of the Southwest* (Orlando, Fla.: Academic Press, 1984). William H. McNeill's overview of the role of disease in human history, *Plagues and Peoples* (New York: Doubleday, 1977), adds much to our understanding of illness in the prehistoric Americas and of how the arrival of Europeans, and with them new viruses, reshaped the continent.

Many books have been written on the indigenous peoples of the Southwest, from Carlos Castaneda's fawning, wildly popular, and entirely mendacious accounts of the supposedly Yaqui sorcerer Don Juan to narrowly academic studies. For the Apache, I have consulted Keith Basso's fine book *Western Apache Language and Culture* (Tucson: University of Arizona Press, 1989); John Gregory Bourke's moving memoir *On the Border with Crook* (New York: Charles Scribner's Sons, 1891); Frank C. Lockwood's interesting but occasionally inaccurate *The Apache Indians* (New York: Macmillan, 1938); Grenville Goodwin's wonderful collection *Myths and Tales of the White Mountain Apache* (New York: American Folklore Society, 1939) and his *Social Organization of the Western Apache* (Chicago: University of Chicago Press, 1942); and Richard J. Perry's modern study *Western Apache Heritage: People of the Mountain Corridor* (Austin: University of Texas Press, 1991). The most useful books on the O'odham are L. S. M. Curtin's *By the Prophet of the Earth: Ethnobotany of the Pima* (Tucson: University of Arizona Press, 1984); Frank Russell's *The Pima Indians* (Washington, D.C.: Bureau of American Ethnology, 1905); George

Webb's remarkable memoir *A Pima Remembers* (Tucson: University of Arizona Press, 1959); and Amadeo Rea's *Once a River: Bird Life and Habitat Changes Along the Middle Gila* (Tucson: University of Arizona Press, 1983), which is as much about the people as the world they once inhabited. Gary Paul Nabhan's *The Desert Smells Like Rain* (San Francisco: North Point Press, 1982) is perhaps the best modern book on the life of the Tohono O'odham; his *Gathering the Desert* (Tucson: University of Arizona Press, 1985) offers well-written over-views of various Southwestern Indian peoples and their use of native plants. Edward F. Castetter and Willis H. Bell's *Yuman Indian Agriculture* (Albuquerque: University of New Mexico Press, 1951), Leslie Spier's *Yuman Tribes of the Gila River* (Chicago: University of Chicago Press, 1933), and Leanne Hinton and Lucille Watahomigie's anthology *Spirit Mountain* (Tucson: University of Arizona Press, 1984) contain important information on the lifeways of the peoples of the lower Gila. For synopses of Southwestern Native American life, see Walter Ebeling's *Handbook of Indian Foods and Fibers of Arid America* (Los Angeles and Berkeley: University of California Press, 1986), and volumes 9 and 10 of the *Handbook of North American Indians* (Washington: Smithsonian Institution Press, 1979), edited by Alfonso Ortiz.

The Spanish arrival in the Americas is also the subject of many books. I have benefited from A. René Barbosa-Ramírez's *La estructura económica de Nueva España, 1519–1810* (México, D.F.: Siglo Veintiuno Editores, 1971); Francisco Almada's *Diccionario de historia, geografía, y biografía sonorenses* (Hermosillo: Estado de Sonora, 1952); Herbert Eugene Bolton's *Rim of Christendom* (New York: Macmillan, 1936), the standard biography of Eusebio Francisco Kino, and his *Spanish Exploration in the Southwest, 1542–1706* (New York: Charles Scribner's Sons, 1916); Alvar Nuñez Cabeza de Vaca's lovely if highly inventive memoir *Adventures in the Unknown Interior of America* (New York: Collier, 1960), in Cyclone Covey's translation; Pedro de Castañeda's *The Coronado Expedition, 1540–1542* (Washington: United States Government Printing Office, 1896), translated by George Parker Winship; Elliott Coues's edition of Francisco Garcés's diaries, *On the Trail of a Spanish Pioneer* (New York: Francis P. Harper, 1900); Charles Gibson's *Spain in America* (New York: Harper & Row, 1966); Eusebio Francisco Kino's *Plan for the Development of Pimería Alta, Arizona, and Upper California* (Tucson: Arizona Pioneers' Historical Society, 1961), translated and annotated by Ernest J. Burrus, S.J.; James Officer's highly useful *Hispanic Arizona* (Tucson: University of Arizona Press, 1986); Ignaz Pfefferkorn's *Sonora: A Description of the Province* (Albuquerque: University of New Mexico Press, 1949), translated by Theodore E. Treutlein; and Herman J. Viola and Carolyn Margolis's *Seeds of Change* (Washington: Smithsonian Institution Press, 1991), a lively account of the introduction of Native American foodstuffs to Europe and vice versa that may profitably be read alongside Alfred W. Crosby's *Ecological Imperialism: The Biological Expansion of Europe, 900-1900* (New York: Cambridge University Press, 1986). David J. Weber's *The Spanish Frontier in North America* (New Haven, Conn.: Yale University Press, 1993) will likely be the standard history well into the next millennium.

The Anglo conquest of the Southwest has given rise to the region's greatest novel, Cormac McCarthy's *Blood Meridian* (New York: Alfred A. Knopf, 1985), which in turn derives much of its dark tale from Samuel E. Chamberlain's memoir *My Confession: The Recollections of a Rogue* (New York: Harper and Brothers, 1956). James Ohio Pattie's story can be found in his *Personal Narrative* (Lincoln: University of Nebraska Press, 1984 [1826]). The lives of other mountain men are related in Bil Gilbert's *Westering Man: The Life of Joseph Reddeford Walker* (New York: Atheneum, 1983) and William Cochran

McGaw's *Savage Scene: The Life and Times of Mountain Man James Kirker* (San Lorenzo, N.M.: High-Lonesome Books, 1988). Accounts of early Anglo exploration and settlement can be found in John Woodhouse Audubon's *Western Journal, 1849–1850* (Cincinnati: Arthur H. Clark and Company, 1905); Mary Austin's *Land of Journeys' Ending* (London: George Allen & Unwin, 1924); Bernard De Voto's *The Year of Decision, 1846* (New York: Little, Brown and Company, 1942); Benjamin Butler Harris's *The Gila Trail*, edited by Richard H. Dillon (Norman: University of Oklahoma Press, 1960); John Russell Bartlett's *Personal Narrative of Explorations and Incidents in Texas, New Mexico, California, Sonora, and Chihuahua* (New York: D. Appleton & Company, 1854); J. Ross Browne's *Adventures in the Apache Country* (New York: Harper & Brothers, 1869); Raphael Pumpelly's *Across Asia and America* (London: Hodder, 1862); and Wallace Stegner's *Beyond the Hundredth Meridian* (Boston: Houghton Mifflin, 1953). On Mormons in Arizona, see Leonard J. Arrington and Davis Bitton's *The Mormon Experience: A History of the Latter-Day Saints* (New York: Alfred A. Knopf, 1979); Robert Gottlieb and Peter Wiley's *America's Saints: The Rise of Mormon Power* (San Diego: Harcourt Brace Jovanovich, 1984); Richard H. Jackson's unpublished doctoral dissertation "Myth and Reality: Environmental Perception of the Mormons, 1840–1865" (Worcester, Mass.: Clark University, 1970); and Virginia Sorensen's charming book of memoirs *Where Nothing Is Long Ago: Memories of a Mormon Childhood* (New York: Harcourt, Brace & World, Inc., 1963). On the Anglo settlement of the Gila headwaters I have drawn from James A. McKenna's *Black Range Tales* (Chicago: Rio Grande Press, 1965) and Marc Simmons's *New Mexico: An Interpretive History* (New York: W.W. Norton, 1977). Dan Thrapp's three-volume *Encyclopedia of Frontier Biography* (Glendale, Calif.: Arthur H. Clark Co., 1988), reprinted in an inexpensive paperback edition by the University of Nebraska Press, is a highly useful reference on all aspects of Southwestern history. So, too, is Richard White's authoritative survey *It's Your Misfortune and None of My Own: A New History of the American West* (Norman: University of Oklahoma Press, 1991).

On Anglo economies, I have used Frank Love's *Mining Camps and Ghost Towns* (Los Angeles: Westernlore Press, 1974); Orson W. Israelsen and Vaughn E. Hansen's *Irrigation Principles and Practices* (New York: John Wiley and Sons, 1962); Carey McWilliams's *Ill Fares the Land: Migrants and Migratory Labor in the United States* (Boston: Little, Brown and Company, 1944); Lynn Jacob's *Waste of the West: Public Lands Ranching* (Tucson: privately printed, 1991); Perri Knize's article "The Mismanagement of the National Forests" in the *Atlantic Monthly* of October 1991; Carsten Lien's *Olympic Battleground: The Power Politics of Timber Preservation* (San Francisco: Sierra Club Books, 1991); R. H. Ring's series "Taming the Forests" in the *Arizona Daily Star*, February 5–12, 1984; and Richard E. Hinton's indispensable *Hand-book to Arizona* (San Francisco: Payot and Upham, 1878).

Many good books and monographs have been devoted to the environments of the greater Southwest. For this book I have found the most useful to be Donald Culross Peattie's *A Natural History of Western Trees* (Boston: Houghton Mifflin, 1991); David Petersen's *Among the Aspen* (Flagstaff, Arizona: Northland Press, 1991); Theodore F. Rixon's *Forest Conditions in the Gila River Forest Reserve, New Mexico* (Washington: U.S. Geological Survey Professional Paper No. 39. Government Printing Office, 1905); David A. Brown and Neil B. Carmony's *Gila Monster* (Silver City, N.M.: High-Lonesome Books, 1991); Charles Lowe's survey *Arizona's Natural Environment* (Tucson: University of Arizona Press, 1964); James A. MacMahon's field guide *Deserts* (New York: Alfred A. Knopf, 1985); Stephen Trimble's *The Sagebrush Ocean: A Natural History of the Great Basin* (Reno: University of Nevada Press, 1989); James Rodney Hastings and Raymond M. Turner's invaluable study *The Changing Mile* (Tucson: University of Arizona Press, 1959); Peter Matthiessen's *Wildlife in America* (New York: Viking Press, 1959); Eugene P. Odum's *Ecology and Our Endangered Life-Support Systems* (Sunderland, Mass.: Sinauer Associates, Inc., 1989); Max Oelschlaeger's philosophical survey *The Idea of Wilderness* (New Haven: Yale University Press, 1991); Jonathan D. Sauer's masterful collection of essays on *Plant Migration* (Berkeley and Los Angeles: University of California Press, 1988); Raymond M. Turner's *Quantitative and Historical Evidence of Vegetation Changes Along the Upper Gila River, Arizona* (Washington: U.S. Geological Survey Professional Paper 655-H. Government Printing Office, 1974); Kenneth D. Frederick and Roger A. Sedjo's edited volume *America's Renewable Resources* (Washington: Resources for the Future, 1991); Donald Worster's *Nature's Economy: A History of Ecological Ideas* (Cambridge: Cambridge University Press, 1976); and especially Frederick R. Gehlbach's *Mountain Islands and Desert Seas: A Natural History of the U.S.-Mexican Borderlands* (College Station: Texas A&M University Press, 1981).

Aldo Leopold's life and work are memorialized in his collections of essays *A Sand County Almanac* (New York: Oxford University Press, 1949) and *The River of the Mother of God* (Madison: University of Wisconsin Press, 1991), edited by Susan L. Flader and J. Baird Caldicott. The definitive biography is Curt Meine's *Aldo Leopold: His Life and Work* (Madison: University of Wisconsin Press, 1988).

Wilderness preservation has a library of its own. The collected nonfiction of Edward Abbey is a starting point, particularly his *Desert Solitaire* (New York: Lippincott, 1968). Another valuable voice is that of environmental journalist Michael Frome; see his recent book *Regreen-*

ing the National Parks (Tucson: University of Arizona Press, 1991) and *Whose Woods These Are: The Story of the National Forests* (Garden City, N.Y.: Doubleday & Company, 1962). Frank J. Popper and Deborah E. Popper have formulated their controversial proposal for a Buffalo Commons in several publications; a useful précis is their article "The Reinvention of the American Frontier" in the *Amicus Journal* of Summer 1991.

ACKNOWLEDGMENTS

This book came into being as the glimmer of an idea conceived at the Moab, Utah, home of Tom and Carolyn Cartwright, in the shadow of the ever-inspiring mountain Tukanikavits. For their generous hospitality I thank Tom and Carolyn, along with Steve and Susan Prescott.

In the form of a proposal, the manuscript made its way to my editor, Steve Topping, at the suggestion of our mutual friend Kim Long. I owe many thanks to both Kim and Steve for their kindness and encouragement, and to Steve for the care and feeding of this book. For other kinds of moral support, I am grateful to Jim Harrison, Barry Lopez, David Quammen, Doug Peacock, and Bernard L. Fontana.

My father, Martin McNamee, and my friend Mark Weiss traveled separate halves of the Gila River with me during the inclement months of February and March 1992, asking good and useful questions during our days on the road. (Merle Haggard, Waylon Jennings, Willie Nelson, Gram Parsons, The Pogues, and The Clash provided the soundtrack for our travels.) David Jones worked wonders as a research assistant; M. H. Salmon, Larry Evers, Peter Warshall, Edison Cassadore, Randy Showstack and Gail Peters of American Rivers,

Charles Bowden, Gary Paul Nabhan, Ofelia Zepeda, Mark Pry, Doug Kupel, Keith Basso, and Julian Hayden provided useful and often hard-to-come-by information of many kinds.

For their help in commenting on the manuscript at several stages, I thank Thomas E. Sheridan, R. H. Ring, Chilton Williamson, Jr., Robert McCord, and John Carpenter. For providing artwork, I thank W. Eugene Hall, Steve Johnson, Lynn Jacobs, Donald B. Sayner, Marshall Trimble of the Southwest Studies Program at Maricopa Community College, Heather Hatch of the Arizona Historical Society, Evelyn Cooper of the Arizona Historical Foundation, and Kathy Hubenschmidt and Helga Teiwes of the Arizona State Museum.

Finally, thanks to my wife, Melissa McCormick, for putting up with the strain of yet another book in the making, and for her unstinting love.

INDEX

DATE